PROBLEMS OF PEACE

TWELFTH SERIES

*Particulars of the previous series appear at
the end of this volume*

PROBLEMS OF PEACE
TWELFTH SERIES

GENEVA AND THE DRIFT TO WAR

by

SIR NORMAN ANGELL

J. B. CONDLIFFE

MALCOLM DAVIS

G. P. GOOCH

CARTER GOODRICH

JACQUES KAYSER

M. D. MACKENZIE

EDGAR A. MOWRER

ANDREW ROTHSTEIN

*This book is based upon lectures given at the Geneva Institute
of International Relations, August 1937, and is published for
the Committee of the Institute*

Essay Index Reprint Series

 BOOKS FOR LIBRARIES PRESS
FREEPORT, NEW YORK

First Published 1938

Reprinted 1970

Particulars of the short annual session of the Institute to be held from 14 to 20 August, 1938, may be obtained from:

The Honorary Secretary, Geneva Institute of International Relations, 15, Grosvenor Crescent, London, S.W.1 ;

The League of Nations Association of the United States, 6, East 39th Street, New York City, U.S.A., and the Director of the Geneva Office, Geneva Institute of International Relations, Club Internationale, 4, rue Adhemar-Fabri, Geneva.

The principal subject for discussion will be 'National Policies and International Organization.'

STANDARD BOOK NUMBER:
8369-1610-7

LIBRARY OF CONGRESS CATALOG CARD NUMBER:
74-111833

PRINTED IN THE UNITED STATES OF AMERICA

EDITOR'S NOTE

EVERY year the Geneva Institute of International Relations holds a public stock-taking of the main movements of international life. To this annual session in Geneva it brings men and women from all parts of the world to pool the results of their studies in international affairs, their experience of international administration, or their personal knowledge of international politics. This volume is based on the work of the session which met in Geneva in August 1937, and is the twelfth to be published by the Institute under the general title PROBLEMS OF PEACE.

Much has been written of the so-called Geneva atmosphere. It is sometimes alleged to be little more than a facile optimism which refuses to face facts, but there is no make-believe about the Institute's discussions, and Captain Walters, the Under Secretary-General of the League of Nations, does not shirk to say, in his Introduction to the present volume, that the moment is more serious than any since the end of the Great War. Indeed, he admits the possibility that the League may cease to exist in its present form, although he personally believes this to be improbable.

The contributors examine the contemporary world, the international repercussions of the Spanish conflict, the malaise in economic co-operation, and analyse critically the reasons for the breakdown of the collective system. The latter part of the book is mainly devoted to the possibilities of establishing satisfactory machinery for peaceful change and to proposals for the formation of a peace front, which are considered in relation to British, French and Soviet foreign policies. Two chapters—dealing with world co-operation on health and with social and economic changes in the United States—suggest that the world has not yet lost the power to direct its own affairs if only it will make up its mind to do so.

The Institute is an entirely impartial body existing simply to promote the study of international questions in what is still by far the best centre for such work. It takes no responsibility for the views expressed by the contributors to this book, but believes that their papers deserve to be studied by a much wider public than had the opportunity to hear them in Geneva.

EDITOR

CONTENTS

Contents

Contents

CHAPTER I

INTRODUCTION

by

FRANK P. WALTERS

Under Secretary-General, League of Nations

YOU have come to Geneva at a time when the international sky is dark. I do not believe that there is an immediate danger of European war—yet I recognize that the moment is a more serious one than any since the end of the Great War. As a simple illustration of that, consider what is being done all over the world now in the matter of armaments. Just about a year ago, all over this little country of Switzerland, the church bells were rung one morning. The national achievement which was celebrated by that ringing of the church bells was the fact that the country had subscribed voluntarily a loan amounting to about 330 million Swiss francs to spend on armaments: that is, that the population of this small country, not much more than half the population of London, and certainly infinitely inferior in wealth, had subscribed a sum of something like 20 million pounds to spend on armaments for the defence of this country. In a few years the whole produce of that enormous sum will have disappeared; all that will remain will be the burden of debt which has to be carried. That achievement was greeted by the ringing of church bells. Now, consider what that means. Consider, too, that at home in England we are going to spend in the next five years

1

1500 million pounds: every year, that is, we spend one and a half times the whole pre-War budget of the country on nothing but armaments, on things which disappear, and in a few years no trace is left. That shows the gravity of the situation and, to be very frank, I want to say straight away that up to the present the League has failed to carry out the main purpose with which it was established, namely, the purpose of getting rid of the fear of war for the future, by the certainty that any country which started war would find itself effectively opposed by all, or the great majority, of the others.

In spite of many partial successes and of many eminent achievements, the efforts of the League in its essential aspect have up to the present failed. Now, I have to begin with that very plain statement, because it forms really the background of all the studies which follow here. The problems to be considered have to be dealt with and solved on the basis of that background of fact. They are not theoretical questions, they are most directly practical questions which affect very immediately and directly the lives of every citizen. You will very often hear people say: 'The League has failed, but that doesn't matter to me,' and, indeed, you too often hear people say: 'The League has failed and I am delighted.' Believe me, anybody who talks like that doesn't know in the least what he is talking about. The failure of the League is not a theoretical event; it is a failure in the essential policy of the States which are members of the League, and the effect of their failure, if it goes too far, is catastrophe and disaster for the citizens of all those States, and just as much of States which are not members of the League.

I expect some of you see sometimes the cartoons of Low

in the *Evening Standard*. I think of one in which he represents a group of countries as a group of five or six people sailing in an open boat on a very rough-looking sea, and this group is divided into two smaller groups, one at each end of the boat. Two or three of these people at one end are baling out the water which is coming in through a hole in the boat, and the two or three at the other end are sitting back very comfortably, saying: 'Thank goodness the hole is not at our end!' That is just as practical as is the attitude of people talking about the failure of the League and saying that it doesn't matter to them. If the League has failed it is going to affect all of them, and they are being exactly what they are very fond of saying that supporters of the League are, namely, pure theorists, who take no account of the real facts.

Does it follow from what I have said either that we *ought* to give up the idea of the League, or that we must reluctantly admit that we *have* to give it up? I do not believe either of those conclusions follows at all, and I shall try and explain very shortly why.

I believe in fact that the League ought to be maintained, that it can be maintained, and that in all probability it will be maintained. The root idea of the League represents an inevitable, necessary, and right development of the political progress of the human race. What is that root idea? We hear of international co-operation, open and honourable dealings between nations, publicity, and so on. Yes, all those come in, but the root idea, the hard core of the League idea, to my mind is something which is simpler and more concrete than that. In a few words, it is the establishment of the rule of law in the relations between nations. If you take a general view of the political progress through the ages of the human race—the political progress, I say, I am not speaking of its moral progress—essentially that consists of the extension of the rule of law in the relations between individuals and groups. That progress has had its ups and downs. There are at this moment in the world places where retreat seems to have taken the place of advance in that respect, but those retreats are clearly temporary, and the main movement of humanity has been unmistakable. Now, there remains one field of human relations, in a way the greatest of all, in which this advance has not been made, and that is the field of the relations between sovereign States. The Covenant is the first great effort of humanity to cover this essential gap in its political progress. I remember how in one of the great books of antiquity, the Republic of Plato, Socrates sets out to find goodness and justice, and he hasn't got very far in the search for those things before he comes to the conclusion that first he must set up a Constitution, a State, a Republic, in which those virtues can flourish. That is essentially, I think, put in a philosophical way, the same point that I am making about the progress of the rule of law. He had to set up a State in which the rule of law was effective before he could develop those higher and more definitely moral qualities. It is the same thing in the relations between States. The first thing that is essential is to establish definite rules which are followed by States in their relations with one another, and the Covenant is in effect the first great effort of humanity to do that. It is impossible to believe that humanity, having once set its hand to this last and greatest achievement in its political development, will turn back. There will, of course, be temporary failures. One such temporary failure, one very

terrible failure, might be that the League as at present
constituted should cease to exist. That is not impossible,
though I consider it very improbable. But what I think
is impossible is that this great move having once been
started, there will ever be a real turning back until it is
achieved. Should this other thing happen—should it
happen that the League were to disappear, certainly that
would mean a loss of time which it is impossible to reckon,
but which would have to be reckoned, I think, in generations, in the progress which can be made towards that great
ideal. If it does not happen, then I think that even though
my generation should fail, the next generation might do
better.

Now I come to my second point: that is, whether in
fact it is possible and probable that the League in its
present form can be maintained. And in passing I would
like to say that any real system of organized international
relations must take approximately the form which the
League takes under the Covenant. It must include a constitutional system for dealing with disputes and differences
between countries; some form of international assistance
organized beforehand for countries which are the victims
of aggression; and some kind of a fixed centre, fixed constitution, with a Council and Assembly and regular meetings. That is the backbone of the League system, and
that is to my mind the minimum which any real international system must include.

I believe that the League in its present form can in fact,
and will in fact, be maintained, and can be strengthened and
nursed to grow gradually to carry out the main ideal for
which it was originally established, that is to say, to get
rid of the fear of war from the face of the earth. There

are many reasons. It would take far too long for me to
try and go very far into them, and I will confine myself
to one or two. The first is that the Covenant represents
an essential step in human progress, from which there will
be no turning back. That is the first great source of
vitality, the conscience which is held by the vast majority
of thinking people all over the world, that the League
system ought to be maintained. The second is the great
achievements and activities which it has in fact carried
out during the fifteen years of its existence.

I will give one example of this vitality of the League—
an example drawn from the relations between the League
and a very interesting and attractive group of the human
race, the Moslem world. Five years ago there were only
two Moslem States which were members of the League—
Persia, which we now call Iran, and the tiny European
State of Albania. They represented a very small pro-
portion of the great Moslem group. Now the membership
of the League includes, besides those two, Turkey, Iraq,
Afghanistan, Egypt. It will include in another two or
three years the new State of Syria, and possibly a new Arab
State of Palestine. In other words, already the great
majority of the Moslem world of its own accord has decided
to join the League. Not only that, but within the last
few days they have signed at the capital of Persia a Treaty
which they have based from beginning to end on the
Covenant. I will not go into details of this agreement,
but I will just draw attention to two points: first, the
Treaty lays down that if any of the parties to the Treaty
—that is, Turkey, Iraq, Iran, and Afghanistan—considers
itself to be the object of aggression, it shall immediately
lay the question before the Council of the League of

Nations; and second, which is perhaps still more remarkable, it was agreed that there should be an annual meeting of the leaders, of the Foreign Ministers, of these four countries in Geneva at the seat of the League. This is a spontaneous act, inspired by no Great Powers, an act taken on their own initiative by the countries concerned—countries which are not considered to be amongst the most advanced, which are not of a very sentimental turn of mind, which have no advantage whatever to gain from a theoretical adhesion to the principles of the League which they don't mean, and I think that it would be difficult to find a more eloquent proof of the fact that the principles of the League and the constitution and actual working of the League maintain a very great vitality in the world in spite of the difficulties and discouragements of recent years.

In conclusion, I would emphasize this point: that the League should always be regarded in terms of business, not of theoretical speculations as to what constitutional arrangements between States might be conceived. The League was formed and shaped out of the colossal pressures of the Great War. If it were to disappear, it would not be replaced by something better or more easily worked, or something theoretically imagined, without some tremendous pressure of the same kind. All that can be done to improve the working of the League must be done on the basis of the League as it exists. It is no use, it is waste of time, to talk about what might be imagined or invented on a basis quite different from this. We are dealing with practical problems to which no effect can be given except by the agreement of the vast majority of the Governments of the countries of the world.

What do we mean when we speak of Peace? Unless we take the trouble to analyse the real meaning of the word, are we not a little apt to think of it merely as a picture—a picture, say, of a summer evening in the country, extending over the whole world, and representing a scene in which the weather is always fine, the crops are good, and all the individuals in sight are provided with an income which is adequate to their desires? That is indeed what peace ought to be, and what perhaps some long time hence it will be. But it is very far from being a picture of what peace in our time can possibly represent. Do not let us think of peace as being a natural condition of things which can be trusted to continue of its own accord so long as no State is wicked enough to upset it. It is something very different from that; something dynamic, not static. It is a great, continuous, I might almost say violent, effort of balance and adjustment between constantly changing stresses, stresses which are due to the unceasing changes in power or population, in sentiment, desire, or temper, amongst the nations of the world. If that effort is to have a chance of success, it cannot be based on improvisation designed to meet each new crisis. Improvisation may be successful once or twice, but to have a real chance of lasting success you must have a system agreed on beforehand between the nations, which covers at least the general principles and the method of procedure which will be followed in every case. And this system, as I have said, cannot be any other than the system of the Covenant.

GENEVA
August 16th, 1937

CHAPTER II

1936–7, A SURVEY

by

Dr. G. P. GOOCH

Author 'History of Modern Europe,' Joint-Editor 'British Documents on the Origins of the War'

MY task is to summarize the crowding events which have occurred since the last meeting of our Institute in August 1936. As usual, it has been a year of unceasing anxiety and recurring alarms. We seem to be living on the slopes of an active volcano, and from time to time we feel the ground trembling under our feet. The most important incidents are the Spanish War, the rearming of Great Britain, the creation of what Mussolini describes as the Rome-Berlin axis, and the renewal of the struggle between China and Japan. I shall have something to say about each of these in due course.

i. *The Far East*

Beginning our long journey in the Far East we note in the first place the signing of the German-Japanese treaty in November 1936, the object of which was to combat Communism at home and abroad. Since this was precisely what the Governments of both countries had been doing with the greatest zeal for several years, the world wondered if that was the whole story. Were there some secret articles, or some unwritten understanding, of a military

9

character inspired by common hostility to Russia? The secret, if there is a secret, is known only to a few individuals in Tokio and Berlin. But there is no mystery about the fact that the two countries are closer to one another than they have ever been.

More recent and far more sensational is the opening of a new phase in the conflict between China and Japan which has raged since the rape of Manchuria in 1931. There is no more tragic chapter in my story to-day than that of the latest attempt to check the progress of a great, industrious, civilized and unmilitary nation. The advance of China in every department of corporate life during the last decade impresses every visitor, and the energy with which such ancient evils as illiteracy and brigandage, famine and flood are being fought deserves our warmest admiration. That her advance is so rapid is clearly one of the reasons which have induced the Japanese militarists to strike, for the longer they wait, the stronger she is likely to become. Now that the puppet State of Manchukuo is firmly established, the great province of Hopei, with Pekin and Tientsin as the plums, lies temptingly near. To dominate the Yangtze region is at present beyond Japan's strength, but the paralysis of the trade of Shanghai by land, sea and air attack facilitates the conquest of the north. Welded by the hammer blows of her implacable foe, China is developing a nationalist fervour which compels Chiang Kai Shek and his colleagues to take up the latest challenge, however unpromising the projects of immediate success. Her best hope lies in Japan's lack of economic resources and financial staying power. Though she won every battle on land and sea in her war with Russia in 1904-5, it was she who secretly asked President

Roosevelt to mediate, since she could no longer bear the strain.

ii. *India—the New Constitution.*

Passing to the centre of the Continent let us linger for a moment in India, where a new constitutional system is about to be tried. Next to the Covenant of the League no political experiment of the last half century is so daring and involves the interests of so many millions. The inauguration of self-government in the Provinces, the sharing of responsibility between the British Raj and the Indian peoples has proceeded by slow stages ever since the Mutiny. But neither the Morley-Minto nor the Montagu-Chelmsford reforms, hotly attacked as they were by the Diehards at the time, compare in significance with the changes which came into operation in the spring of 1937. If there is danger in leaping forward, there is far greater peril in holding back, for 'the patient East' of Matthew Arnold's poem is now as impatient as the West. The deadlock in the six Provinces out of eleven where a Congress majority was returned in the elections of February 1937 has been happily removed by the statesmanship of Gandhi and the Viceroy, and Congress Ministers are now busily at work.

iii. *France Withdraws from Syria.*

At the south-western extremity of Asia two events claim our attention. After a singularly disappointing experience in Syria the French have decided to withdraw. The announcement of their approaching retirement was hailed with delight by the Syrians, with dismay by the Turkish population in the district of Alexandretta. Though not unwilling to be ruled by France, the prospect of living as a powerless minority in an independent Syrian State filled them and their brothers beyond the Taurus mountains with apprehension. For a brief space there was tension between Paris and Angora. But the healing influence of Geneva was applied, and a satisfactory compromise was reached by which the Turks of Alexandretta receive far-reaching autonomous rights within the new State. In a year which has witnessed a further decline in the prestige and vitality of the League, let us not overlook this modest achievement.

iv. *The Anglo-Egyptian Treaty.*

The most notable event in the history of the Dark Continent during the last twelve months is the Anglo-Egyptian treaty which terminates the British Occupation of more than half a century and removes a juristic anomaly. Our presence in the valley of the Nile was neither invited by the Sultan of Turkey, the suzerain of Egypt before the World War, nor approved by the Egyptian people. Repeated attempts since the end of the conflict to reach a settlement broke down on one or other of the points at issue. It was not till Italy's attack on Abyssinia brought home to Egyptian statesmen the danger in which they stood that they reduced their demands and that the difficulties were overcome. The treaty provides for mutual defence for twenty years, for the removal of the British garrison to the Canal, for an Egyptian share in the administration of the Sudan, and for the abolition of the Capitulations. It is a curious illustration of the fact that every move on the world's chessboard leads to unexpected results. That Great Britain has at last been enabled to put herself right with the Egyptian people is due to the Duce alone. Meanwhile it is not all plain sailing in Abyssinia since the flight of the Emperor and the occupation of Addis Ababa, and large parts of the highlands are still unconquered. It is a fairly safe forecast that Mussolini will find his new Empire as difficult to subdue as Algeria, and later Morocco, proved to the French.

v. *America—the New Deal.*

Springing across the Atlantic our eyes are fixed on the striking figure of Franklin Roosevelt, gallantly struggling to compress into his term of office the programme of social reform which should have been carried out in the generation before the great slump in 1929. Called to the helm at a moment when, in his own phrase, America was dying by inches, he breathed new confidence into the nation. In his task of modernizing the capitalistic system and securing a minimum standard of life for the common man, he was bound to incur the savage hostility of Wall Street and the more decorously veiled antagonism of the Supreme Court. His proposal, after his triumphant re-election in November 1936, to rejuvenate that august tribunal by increasing its membership and introducing fresh blood was approved by many who deplored the method he chose, and his plan was rejected by a majority of Senators largely composed of his own party. For the Separation of Powers, which inspired the framers of the Constitution, is still a living tradition. Yet his labours have not been in vain. The decisions of the Court began to show a welcome diminution of rigidity when the campaign was in full swing, and the resignation of one of the old guard among the Justices made room for an ardent supporter of the New Deal. Whichever party or

school of thought within the party wins the next Presidential
election, the main part of the structure is likely to stand ;
for wealthy and civilized communities do not go back on
such indispensable services as old age pensions and insurance
against sickness and unemployment.

vi. *Russia.*

Recrossing the Atlantic let us begin our European
journey with Russia, where a series of mass executions
suggests widespread discontent. The workings of the
Russian mind are never easy to follow, and it is particularly
difficult to interpret the ferocious campaign against what
is called Trotzkyism. Is it merely a personal struggle for
power between Stalin and the remnants of the old guard,
or is it a conflict between rival policies? Were Tuta-
chevsky and the seven other Generals shot because Stalin,
anticipating a challenge to his omnipotence, got his blow
in first? Or were they the victims of their desire to get
into friendly touch with the chiefs of the German army?
The charge of desiring the invasion, defeat and dismember-
ment of their own country is of course ridiculous. But did
they dream of a *détente* which would remove, or at any
rate diminish, the danger of war? Explanations and
assurances, we were informed, were sent to France and
Czechoslovakia, who are Russia's allies; but we have not
been let into the secret. Whether the morale of the army
and therefore its military value has suffered from the
execution of men who have laboured to make it what it is
we cannot be sure, for the only reliable test of fighting
quality is war. What cannot be doubted is the nervous-
ness and the ruthlessness of the Dictator, the existence of

widespread discontent, and the complete uncertainty in the army and the administration whose turn to face the firing-squad will come next. Such savagery is not calculated to increase the popularity of the alliance in France, or to strengthen the cohesion of what some people envisage as the new Triple Entente.

vii. *Poland.*

The problems of Poland during the last twelve months, like those of Russia, have been domestic rather than foreign. She has profited less by the world economic revival than most countries, and the continuing poverty of the people has bred both political discontent and a virulent anti-Semitism. Unlike Germany, where the campaign against the Jews is directed by the Government, Marshal Smigly-Rydz and the men who enjoy his confidence are relatively free from this distressing ailment. It rages among students in the Universities, who scent dangerous competitors in the struggle for life, and among the peasants, who in their distress instinctively go for the nearest Jew as the symbol of sinister forces which they do not understand.

The tightening of the ties between Warsaw and Bucharest is the main feature of the foreign relations of Poland in the last year. The object of the alliance is to diminish the chances of war in Eastern Europe by establishing a sort of buffer from the Baltic to the Black Sea, separating Germany from Russia and Russia from her Czechoslovak allies. Since the dismissal of the Francophile Titulesco in the summer of 1936 Roumania's policy is believed to have become rather more Germanophile, and indeed German influence, political, economic and cultural, has steadily

increased in the Balkans in recent months But whoever
makes trouble in that quarter it will not be the country
which realized the whole of its territorial ambition in the
World War and only desires to keep what it has got.

viii. *Greece.*

In Greece the Metaxas dictatorship inaugurated by his
coup of August 4, 1936, has failed to restore harmony or
prosperity. The drachma has fallen, the prisons are filled
with critics or suspects, the Press is muzzled, Government
propaganda is rampant, letters are opened, telephones are
tapped.   How familiar is the technique of autocracy nowadays! The record of previous *coups* leads us to hope that
the present detestable and incompetent regime will not
last very long. The ambitious General may be over-
thrown by another soldier, or the King may intervene
when he believes the hour has come, as King Alfonso dis-
missed Primo da Rivera when his popularity had ebbed.
The Greeks are notoriously a critical race, and the inability
of the two dominant Parliamentary groups to form a stable
government played into the hands of Metaxas. The
moral of the story is that the parties must display a greater
spirit of compromise if the constitutional government
desired by the overwhelming majority of a highly educated
and liberty-loving community is to return and endure.

ix. *The Balkans.*

The most notable recent events in the Balkans are Jugoslavia's treaties of friendship with Bulgaria and Italy. The
rapprochement between Sofia and Belgrad, inaugurated

before the murder of King Alexander and involving the tacit renunciation by Bulgaria of her claims to Macedonia, reached its final stage in the agreement of January 1937. Written declarations of goodwill and good intentions are only of value when they correspond to the sentiment and interests of the signatories. Tried by this test the treaty may be welcomed by us all. Slowly and reluctantly Bulgaria has come to realize that she is too weak to regain the coveted province for which she fought in 1913 and for which she entered the World War in 1915, and that nobody is likely to help her. Politics, as Bismarck used to say, are the art of the possible. Of the subsequent treaty with Italy it is difficult to speak so confidently. That the fierce enmity of the post-War years has given place to confidence and friendship nobody believes. Albania remains an apple of discord, and the unchallenged domination of the Adriatic by the Italian fleet is not at all to the taste of Belgrad. The agreement is a *détente*, not an *entente*. How deep is the suspicion of Italy may be seen in the violent resistance to the Government's recent concessions to the Roman Catholic members of the State, in which not only the Orthodox Church but many ardent Serb patriots detected a potential increase of Italian influence.

x. *Hungary.*

The current of Hungary's life has flowed more smoothly since the death of Gömbös a year ago, for the General was moving steadily towards a dictatorship on the model of Berlin, with which he was in close contact. His successor Daranyi, who was expected to be merely a stop-gap, has strengthened his position by his moderation and his readiness to co-operate with Count Bethlen and other leaders. No Hungarian will surrender the hope of territorial revision; but there is a time for everything, and Daranyi is not the man to force the pace.

xi. *Austria.*

In Austria the barometer has been less steady. Dr. Schuschnigg maintains his uneasy position as a quasi-Dictator who knows that an appeal to the country would sweep him away. Yet it is precisely the inability of the Socialists and the Nazis to combine which enables him to survive. The truce between Berlin and Vienna established in July 1936, by which Hitler purchased Mussolini's friendship at the price of postponing his Austrian ambitions, is admittedly an experiment. The Austrian Nazis are by no means disposed to play the passive *rôle* assigned to them in that transaction, and their feud with the Government breaks out in occasional demonstrations and incidents. The economic situation is a little easier. Meanwhile the Archduke Otto bides his time.

xii. *Germany.*

When France has a cold, observed Metternich a century ago, all Europe sneezes. Today it is Germany, not France, to which all eyes are anxiously turned. In the domestic field the two main features of the story are the worsening of the economic situation and the intensification of the campaign against the Churches. There is little unemployment, thanks to re-armament and public works; but the effort to achieve self-sufficiency, commonly known as autarchy or ecomonic nationalism, involves a diminution of the amenities of life. Deficits accumulate, and the people are not allowed to know the amount. All that one man can do has been done by the resourceful Dr. Schacht; but the question is often asked inside Germany as well as outside, How long can the rake's progress go on? The attack on the Churches astonishes the world, which watches the stoutest enemies of Communism being turned into angry critics of the Nazi regime. The arrest of Pastor Niemöller and dozens of other honoured preachers has revealed the Nazi chiefs as the enemies of Christianity no less than of political and intellectual liberty. So long as the army stands by the dictator, the regime is safe from internal revolt. But the volume of criticism steadily increases, even in the land described long ago by Herder as *terra obedientiae*. After a time most civilized people tire of being treated like children.

No sensational event occurred in Germany's foreign relations between the summers of 1936 and 1937. The seizure of Danzig is no longer feared, not only because the goodwill of Poland is needed, but because the old Hanse city has become Nazi in fact if not in name. The High Commissioner of the League is more like a prisoner than an arbiter, and the minority parties have been ruthlessly eliminated. With Czechoslovakia relations have been more strained than ever. The belated concessions to the German minority in the north, made by Prague in February 1936, have done little to mitigate the discontent of the Henlein party, which increasingly turns its eyes towards Berlin. That Czechoslovakia is the ally of Russia is a further cause of suspicion and resentment to the Nazis, who fill their Press with baseless stories of Russian pilots and aerodromes on their southern frontier.

Germany's partnership with Italy, arising from the re-
alignment of the Powers in consequence of the Abyssinian
war, developed rapidly in the period under review. Beginning with Austria it extended to Spain, where the two
Powers recognized Franco at an early stage of his revolt,
and where they have throughout striven to secure his
victory. For the installation of a Fascist dictator in
Madrid, owing his place to the aid of Hitler and Mussolini,
would not only be a triumph for the anti-democratic forces
which they represent, but would weaken the position of
France in the western Mediterranean. By the creation of
the Rome-Berlin axis Hitler has escaped from moral and
material isolation. Ten years ago he declared in *Mein
Kampf* that Germany's first task was to recover her strength,
and prophesied that, when she had done so, she should be
able to find an ally in Italy or England for the realization
of her ambitions. It was a remarkable forecast.

xiii. *France.*

The Italo-German partnership has inevitably increased
the apprehensions of France. So clear seemed the danger
that the Front Populaire, with Blum at its head, hurried
on the organization of national defence as zealously as any
Government of the Centre or Right. It was equally inevitable that the bonds between Paris and London should
be drawn ever tighter as Germany grew daily in armed
strength and freedom of manœuvre. In a world of flux,
when old friends become foes and old foes turn overnight
into friends, the rock-like solidity of the Anglo-French
partnership stands out in bold relief. The colossal rearmament programme, adopted by the British Parliament

with little opposition, is at once an evidence of our anxieties and an affirmation of our resolve to defend our interests. England and France, as we all know, are pledged to aid one another in the event of an unprovoked German attack, and both have undertaken to succour Belgium in a similar emergency. Outside the Locarno bloc in its new form (with three members instead of five) the British Government continues to keep a free hand, neither promising to come in to a conflict nor to stay out. To the complaint that such an attitude is unworthy of a Great Power and encourages Fascist dictators to take risks, we can only reply that a stronger policy would be difficult to adopt in view of the profound division of opinion as to what we ought to do.

xiv. *Spain—The Civil War.*

If the Abyssinian war was the main event of 1935-6, the civil war in Spain dominates the story of 1936-7. The recent history of that country since the war fills her many friends with sadness. If the Parliamentary system was a failure, what else can be said of Primo's dictatorship, mild though it was? His fall dragged down the Monarch and the Monarchy, and the Republic was suddenly faced with the task of building a new Spain. Here again was disappointment. After winning the elections of 1931 the Left pushed boldly ahead with plans for agricultural and educational reform, while at the same time it secured the contentment of Catalonia by the grant of far-reaching autonomy. But its pace was too hot for the conservative republicans, and its anti-clerical measures alienated the sentiments of large sections of a community with a long catholic tradition. The swing of the pendulum in 1933

brought to power the Centre-Right, as Professor Allison
Peers calls it in his excellent book, *The Spanish Tragedy*.
But if the Left seemed to move too fast, their successors
marched too slow. Forgetting the wise maxim of Lord
John Russell that there is nothing so conservative as progress, they halted the reforms and offered nothing in their
place. Exasperation found vent in rebellions in Catalonia
and the Asturias, the ruthless repression of which sent the
pendulum swinging back towards the Left. The elections
of February 1936 revealed the country divided into two
almost equal camps, the Left, or Popular Front, ranging
from academic Liberals to Communists, securing a majority
of seats, its opponents a small majority of votes.

The first task of Azana, the outstanding figure of the
Left, on returning to office, was to resume the application
of the reforms inaugurated in 1931–3. But his task was
hopeless from the outset, and on his promotion to the
Presidency of the Republic his influence withered away.
His opponents were far more united than his supporters,
and the forces of anarchy began to get out of control. The
Government, well-meaning but lamentably weak, proved
unable either to carry out the urgently needed agrarian
reforms at the rapid pace demanded by an impatient
peasantry living at a semi-starvation level, or to prevent
the miscellaneous assassinations which indicate the gathering
of a storm. The murder of Calvo Sotelo, the strong man
of the Right, in revenge for the murder of an officer of the
militia, started the avalanche. General Franco raised the
standard of revolt in Spanish Morocco in July 1936, encouraged by Italy, whence military aeroplanes had arrived,
and whence tens of thousands of troops were to follow.
The carefully planned rebellion in which the larger part

of the army was involved, broke out in the chief towns and Garrisons of Spain. In Madrid and Barcelona it was promptly suppressed by the almost unarmed manual workers.

Despite this disappointment Franco's troops marched rapidly north, took Badajoz and Toledo, and at the end of October were at the gates of Madrid. At this moment, when the capital was expected to fall, the advance guard of the International Brigade, consisting of volunteers from many countries, marched through the streets, bringing fresh hope to the supporters of the Government. Russian stores of food and munitions poured in through Barcelona, while German aeroplanes and experts reinforced Italy's effort to establish a totalitarian regime. By the end of 1936 the country was divided into two parts, the Government, which had moved to Valencia, holding the territory east of a line drawn roughly from north to south, Franco the territory to the west, in addition to Majorca, where Italy was supreme.

In such a conflict, disgraced by savagery on both sides recalling the atrocities of the Carlist wars, it is far too early to attempt a final judgment. Good and bad men, it is clear, are to be found in both camps. Each side can make out a plausible case for itself. The Government claims that it was returned by a substantial majority at a free election, and that it was striving to carry out reforms which ought to have been introduced long ago. The rebels reply that it could not keep order or guarantee life and property; that power had passed into the hands of socialists, communists, anarchists, and the enemies of religion, and that the revolt merely anticipated an organized massacre of members of the Right. We shall do well to avoid over-simplification. To describe it as a struggle between Fascism and Communism is only partially correct; for Franco has many followers who are not Fascists, and the Government many supporters who are not Communists. To regard it as a war of religion is equally misleading, for the Basque defenders of Bilbao are zealous Catholics. The Church is widely disliked, not for its dogmas, but for its traditional association with the ruling classes and their interests. The average Englishman, whatever his party label, is Left Centre, and his ideal is ordered liberty. Unfortunately there seems no room in Spain today for the moderate man, for both sides are ready to suppress their opponents and to impose their opinions by force. If respect for life and conscience is the real test of civilization, Spain is among the most backward communities in Europe.

At the time of the French Revolution Burke described Jacobinism as an armed doctrine, and we are confronted today, not with one such phenomenon, but with three. To the territorial disagreements resulting from the peace treaties are added ideological differences which cut equally deep. Is the open intervention in Spain of Italy and Germany on one side, and of Russia on the other, a rehearsal of the next world war? Material issues are involved, such as the influence of Italy in the western Mediterranean, and the desire of France to guarantee the unimpeded transport of her troops from Africa. Yet the factors are not wholly material. There is a general doctrinal difference between the champions of authoritarian and libertarian rule—how deep is revealed by the failure of the efforts of the Non-Intervention Committee. Who can span the gulf?

xv. *The Future.*

It is a sign of the tragic impotence of the League that no one seriously expects it to deal with the wars in Spain or China. Our survey of 1936–7 indeed must close on a note of anxiety though by no means of despair. Despite the solemn obligations of the Kellogg Pact, war as an instrument of national policy is as popular as ever, for aggression against weak States seems to pay. Armaments are racing ahead in every country, large and small, and monster battleships, after a blessed interval of sanity, are again floating on the waves. Production throughout the world has increased and unemployment has diminished. The Belgian Premier, Van Zeeland, has been commissioned to sketch out a programme of economic co-operation, and King Leopold has argued for the creation of something like an economic General Staff. But the spirit of association seems lacking : regional pacts, political and otherwise, are preferred to general commitments, and the shadow of war hangs over the world. Since the failure of the Disarmament Conference of 1932 and the World Economic Conference of 1933, statesmen, with the exception of Mr. Lansbury, have lost faith in the healing influence of the round table. It will be for my successor a year hence to relate how the Spanish war ended, how the struggle in the Far East developed, how Europe escaped or failed to escape from the perils that beset us on every side.

CHAPTER III

THE SPANISH CONFLICT: ITS INTERNATIONAL REPERCUSSIONS

by
EDGAR ANSEL MOWRER
Director, Paris Bureau, 'Chicago Daily News'

ALMOST thirteen months ago to a day the lid blew off in Spain. A group of officers, assisted by Monarchists, Fascists, clericals, and rich men, rose against the Republican Government. The greater part of the Spanish army and the police followed their officers in revolt. The rebellion was blessed by the Catholic Hierarchy. Successful in Morocco, Seville, Burgos and Salamanca, the revolt was overcome in the strategic centres of Madrid, Barcelona and Valencia, thus turning an insurrection into a bitter and bloody Civil War.

Significantly enough, the Spanish uprising occurred just two months after the final collapse of Abyssinian resistance, one month after Great Britain announced its readiness to raise the sanctions still feebly operative against Pact-breaking Italy. It almost seemed as though certain people feared any drop in the temperature of the European witches' kettle.

Thanks to immediate foreign intervention, this essentially Spanish affair, the logical outcome of over a century of Spanish history, became not only a conceivable curtain-raiser to a bigger and better European struggle, but itself a sort of European war by proxy. This nominally internal struggle in a single none-too-important country, raised at one time all of the important political issues of contemporary Europe.

i. *Some Personal Impressions.*

My personal experiences of the Spanish struggle were limited to a few weeks. A few days after the outbreak of the rebellion, before train service had been re-established, I walked through the frontier tunnel on the Mediterranean side and was immediately arrested by a shot-gun-waving militiamen in overalls at Port Bou in Spain. I witnessed something of the workmen's attempt to actuate an anarchist or 'libertarian communist' revolution in Catalonia. From a prominent leader of the dreaded F.A.I. or Anarchist Federation at Barcelona, I learned something at first hand of the 'nudism through terror' philosophy that animates so many simple Spaniards, who, having never seen any sort of decent Government or honest administration, have come to identify Heaven with the absence of law. I saw several burned churches and pillaged houses. I saw fascists freshly executed according to the anarchist motto 'Kill without hate.' I watched the anarchists play at war while actually stealing and hoarding arms—and other things as well—according to their theory that 'the goods of all belong to all and to none.'

At Madrid I saw less disorder among the Spaniards than panic among the well-to-do foreigners, even including some diplomats. In a motor-car flying a red flag, labelled 'inspection of militia,' with an overalled bodyguard and chauffeur on the front seat, I went where I pleased along the front from Somosierra to Toledo. I climbed to a roof a hundred yards from the bullet-spitting Alcazar. I hung

about Largo Caballero's labour headquarters at Fuen-
carral 93, talking with Del Vayo and Araquistain and
Caballero himself, with whom I twice went to the front.
When I left Spain I was not entirely convinced that the
Government would win, and for two reasons : First, the
workmen seemed more interested in social reform than in
fighting the rebellious army, and it is at best hard for an
armed population to resist even a Spanish regular army ;
Second, I was not at all sure what sort or what amount
of foreigners General Franco (for General Sanjurjo died
in an aviation accident) would succeed in getting to fight
for him.

Since then I have not been back in Spain. But from
the reports of such Americans as H. R. Knickerbocker, John
Whitaker, Webb Miller, Miss Frances Davis and others
on the Rebel side, and of numerous other friends with the
Loyalists, I have tried to follow events in and concerning
Spain. *The Chicago Daily News* had a correspondent
in Malaga just after it was conquered ; a correspondent
in Portugal and Gibraltar ; it keeps a correspondent in
Madrid with whom I talk almost daily by telephone.

It is on the basis of all this that I give you my
conclusions :   I   am   neither   socialist   nor   communist,
and have been over twenty years a foreign correspondent.
If I have failed to reach the truth, the fault is mine
alone.

My belief is that the present horror in Spain is the result
of an international Fascist conspiracy concocted between
Spanish generals in Spain and dictators in Rome, Berlin
and Lisbon. Without the assistance given the Spanish
rebels by the fascists outside, the insurrection would have
failed within a brief time. Soviet Russia, in my judgment,

had little or no responsibility in the Civil War, and the charge that it has, is, in my opinion, a red herring brought into the picture by the fascists in the hope that its odour will cover the scent of this Fascist Internationale.

ii. *How it came About*

Spain missed the bourgeois era almost altogether. The hope of the Spanish middle class died with the suppression of the *Comuneros* in 1521. At least it never recovered from what it suffered then. Until 1931 the country was feudally governed by a monarchy based on the army, the big landowners, and the Catholic Church. Whether or not it was well governed depends upon one's attitude towards what is called modern enlightenment. In the light of mediæval mysticism the Government may have been a model. Certainly it furthered piety. There was one priest for every nine hundred inhabitants, as against one for every twenty thousand inhabitants in Italy. A huge share of the national wealth was in the hands of the Church. When after 1931 the Republic feebly set about nationalizing the property of the congregations, the Pope declared that the law behind it constituted 'the record of all laws against God and human souls.' And in the catechism used in all Spanish churches until 1936 was the following passage:

'*Question*. What sin is committed by those who vote liberal?

'*Answer*. Usually mortal sin.'

The Church was in charge of practically all education. In 1936 over 45 per cent of the population were still illiterate; half of the children in Madrid could not be educated owing to lack of places, and forty thousand school teachers earned twenty dollars a month, or less.

These details may account for the fact that the national hymn of Catalonia expresses equal hate for 'monks and full bellied young gentlemen'; that in Spain all down the nineteenth and twentieth centuries revolt has meant burned churches and convents. Most churchmen supported a regime that meant privileges for them and 'order, unity, security, decency and good conduct' (Semorun Gurrea, *A Catholic Looks at Spain*).

Spain might be a rich country; actually it has been dreadfully poor. One reason is that a few thousand large landowners possess more than 50 per cent of the land and about 60 per cent of the total national wealth. These owners have more soil than they can cultivate: the rest lies fallow or is used for grazing. Millions of peasants own little or nothing and live on an animal standard. Out of the landowning families come the reactionary bourgeoisie that surprises and delights strangers, for Spaniards are essentially likeable. The upper classes feel the need of a hard hand to protect them against the uprising of a famished people '. . . an iron hand that will close the mouths of the disinherited . . . silence their cries of anguish, their insults, their distress, and, above all, the terrible logic of their protests' (Guerrea).

The third pillar of the monarchical Government was the army officer, until recently one for every five men, drawn from the same social level as the high priests and the land-owners. Spain, be it remembered, escaped the great popular movements of the last hundred years.

It had its own: the account of the *Encyclopedia Britannica* becomes almost monotonous in telling how ever so often the masses revolted and 'the military crushed the rebellion with an iron hand.' In 1823 French soldiers came in to stamp out Spanish Liberalism at the bidding of the Holy Alliance. During the troubled period between 1868 and 1873 the Spanish army, assisted by British and German naval squadrons, restored absolutism. But the efficiency of this army went no further than crushing its own people. In the course of army rule, Spain lost a gigantic colonial empire; was subjected to one long series of foreign humiliations; and was finally defeated, save for French help, by a handful of African tribesmen under Abd-el-Krim. During the world war the Spanish ruling classes were logically pro-German, for they have always sought to preserve their people from heresies like self-government, popular education and a more equitable distribution of property.

The Spanish Republic of 1931 came into power in order to change all this. Bloodlessly, without vengence. It allowed monarchists and churchmen and women to vote. It opened 10,000 new schools. It let the deposed King and the departing nobles take their property away with them. It accepted defeat by the Reactionaries in the 1933 elections. The ultimate aim of the Conservatives (as confessed by their newspaper *El Debate* in 1933) was to get rid of Parliament and democracy altogether. Only after such warnings a few of the more radical miners, fearful of being deprived of what little in the way of democracy and land reform had been accomplished, began an insane insurrection in the Austurias which was shot down by Moors and foreign legionaries in the name of God. There were continual strikes. There was general unrest—as much brawling as in the spring of 1936, although the Conservatives under Calvo Sotelo and Gil Robles were in power. The generals who had revolted against the Republic in 1932 (and been pardoned by the gentle Republicans) were restored to places of trust.

Now, for nearly a century there has been some Socialism in Spain. In 1873 Sevillian Republicans decreed the abolition of private property. In the 1936 election 98 Socialists and 16 Communists were elected out of a total of 473 deputies to the Cortes. Of the two large labour organizations in Spain, one, the u.n.t., was distinctly 'pink,' while the other, the c.n.t., was largely dominated by anarchists. But against 114 Reds, the victorious Popular Front contained 146 bourgeois Liberals, for a total of 268 seats as against 205 for their adversaries. It is true that the Popular Front received 60,000 votes less than that of the combined Centre and Right opposition, just as in 1916 in the United States, Wilson, the winner, received fewer votes than the defeated Hughes. But the election occurred according to rule, and there was no doubt of its legality.

Socialists and anarchists were determined that this time the liberal reforms should be applied to the letter. They pushed for immediate sale of uncultivated land to landless peasants. They demanded army reform and exiled a few of the most recalcitrant generals. They burnt more churches. But the real trouble came from the Right. Sotelo and Gil Robles realized that once the estates were broken up and the army republicanized, their last chance of preventing a Spanish New Deal would be gone. They began to assassinate their adversaries. Killings led to counter-killings. President Azana, gentle as always, did not react with the necessary energy. Meanwhile, the Conservatives found allies in Berlin, Rome and Lisbon. A rebellion was prepared to the slightest details: military uprisings in all the large centres would definitely overthrow the Republic. In its place they would restore the ancient rule in a new Fascist binding. The assassination of their leader Sotelo in revenge for the murder by fascists of a republican police lieutenant merely caused them to let go a little sooner than was expected. And with the cry, 'Spain awake!' they set about saving the Spaniards from democracy with the full help and approval of three foreign Governments and conceivably certain financiers elsewhere. Thanks to the violent reaction of the long-suffering Spanish masses and the utter disorder that resulted, they were able to make themselves popular among world conservatives as the saviours of Spain from 'Bolshevism.' The fact is, however, that the generals, Goded, Sanjurjo, Franco and Cabarellas—who rebelled against the legitimate Government and plunged Spain into the horrors of a Civil War beside which other atrocities are trifles, were precisely those who rose against the Republic in 1932 and belonged to the same groups who had ruled the country for centuries, and made Spain what it was.

That the Franco rebellion failed was due to Spanish workmen in overalls. Spanish sailors killed their disloyal officers, and some of the aviators were faithful. But in the main the workmen did the trick. In Catalonia their movement was cruel and infantile, though not a tenth as cruel or bloody or revolting as was written in the Conservative newspapers the world over. From what I heard in Paris I expected to find the country a shambles. In point of fact, though killings were frequent, the authorities tried to prevent them. On the Rebel side more numerous assassinations were systematically carried out on order from above and blessed by Catholic priests. The Rebels priests.   The Rebels counted on their outcries about burned churches and raped nuns to cover their own wholesale slaughter in places like Badajoz.   For as ex-King Alfonso himself put the matter in an interview to the *London Evening Standard* of July 24, 1936:

> 'In my opinion, only the extermination, once and for all, of the Left Parties, will put an end to this Civil War, and will give Spain the peace so much desired by all true Spaniards.'

The course of the actual fighting is too well known to need description.   Less generally understood is the situation which the repulse of the initial *coup d'état* left on the Loyalist side.   The lower middle class was on the whole favourable to the Government, but it was unorganized, uncertain, local rather than national in allegiance, dismayed by what it saw.   The *Putsch* was put down, not by the bourgeoisie but by the labour organizations.   In nearly every locality it was the U.G.T., or the C.N.T., which provided the overalled workmen who stood up against the mutinous army.   Inevitably labour committees took charge. They used their power not only to defend the Republic, but to carry out a miniature revolution.   As the pro-Moscow writer, Louis Fischer, puts it: 'When the Civil War broke out, many landlords and big business men in loyalist territory fled or were hurriedly tried and executed as fascist sympathizers, or were murdered by peasants in retaliation for years of poverty and subjugation.   Their properties were thereupon confiscated.'   This was practically unavoidable.   For the middle class Cabinet, in which there was not a single socialist, was faced with a choice: either arm the organized workmen at the risk of social disorder or succumb to their ancient enemies.   The Government took the first risk—and saved the Republic, with its liberal democratic constitution and human liberties. Rich men all over the world protested against this: they were prepared to place the rights of property above the rights of man. But President Azana and his friends thought otherwise and counted on the stubborn individualism of the Spaniard to prevent any permanent dominion by collectivist ideas. At most they expected a month or two of disorder, and then, with the rebellion quashed, they could gradually restore a reign of law. They failed to foresee foreign Fascist intervention on a gigantic scale. Without this intervention the rebellion would have collapsed within a few weeks, for, be it said and re-said, the majority of the Spaniards, the vast majority, were against restoration of rule by their former overlords, the army, the Church, and the big landlords.

iii. *Foreign Intervention.*

The Governments of Germany, Italy, and Portugal were determined that the Popular Front Government of Madrid be driven from office by the Spanish Rebels. The facts are not yet entirely clear, but enough is known to leave no doubt of the situation.

German imperialists (particularly of the so-called 'naval school' to which Adolf Hitler is apparently becoming converted), have always seen in Spain the tool for cutting French connexions with its source of military man-power in North Africa. During the World War, Germany twice offered the Germanophile Spanish Government Gibraltar and Portugal if it would enter the war on the side of the Central Empire. The Nazis merely revived this old policy, along with so many other things from Imperial days.

During the Conservative phase of the Spanish Republic, between the elections of 1933 and 1936, they honeycombed Spain with their organizations and agents—hundreds and hundreds of them, from the espionage and kidnapping *Hafendienst,* a camouflaged arm of the *Gestapo* at home, through the Fichte-Bund, to the regular diplomats, who abused diplomatic immunity to distribute propaganda material against Spanish democracy. Tons of their stuff was seized by the Spanish Government after the outbreak of the Civil War, and there is no doubt of the facts.

After the Spanish Popular Front came to power in February 1936, the Germans plotted with the exiled Spanish General Sanjurjo during his stay in Germany in the spring, and unquestionably arranged co-operation and support for the coming rebellion. Immediately after its outbreak, German warships prevented Spanish Government war vessels from bombarding Ceuta in Morocco, when they might have hindered the transport of men and material from Africa to form Franco's army. German aeroplanes, pilots and mechanics, German tanks and tank corps, German artillery and gunners, German war material of all conceivable sorts were soon on the spot. In all some thousands of highly trained German specialists, including strategists and *Reichswehr* officers who did turns of service in the Spanish Foreign Legion, contributed to swell Franco's army. The Spaniards called them 'White Moors.' For the rest, Germany co-operated in everything with Italy.

Italian intervention was even larger, though perhaps less effective. Italian flyers were commandeered for Franco's service two days before the rebellion occurred. Italian planes and pilots carried over from Morocco the 4000 original Moorish veterans who enabled Franco to take the offensive that in three months brought him to the suburbs of Madrid. Italian troops led in the capture of Malaga; were routed at Guadalajara; did fairly well against the badly armed Basques at Bilbao; and together with Moors, Germans and some Spaniards formed what was known paradoxically as the 'Nationalist Army.'

Italian warships did naval intelligence service for the Rebels, helped organize Mallorca and Ibiza in the Balearics, and conceivably, though not surely, went as far as torpedoing Spanish Government ships.

All in all, military assistance to Spain is believed to have cost Germany at least 250 million dollars, and Italy about 150 million.

But if their military assistance was vital, their diplomatic support was hardly less so. In close co-operation with the Portuguese dictator, Salazar, these countries recognized the Insurgents as the legitimate Spanish Government, and under threat of open war, bullied the French and British Governments into changing the current international practice against the lawful Government and in favour of their protégé. Vauntingly they proclaimed that they would 'never permit' a victory of 'Bolshevism'—meaning the Republic—in the Civil War. Temporarily, at least, they created in the Mediterranean a strategic situation extremely dangerous for Great Britain and for France. That they could do this was due to the artifice of the Non-Intervention Committee, one of the most amazing diplomatic hoaxes ever created.

Normally the Spanish Government had a right to purchase war material anywhere in the world and to receive assistance where it liked. In recognition of this right, the French immediately authorized one sale of war aeroplanes, which reached Spain early in August, and were almost immediately put out of commission by incompetent Spanish fliers. But meanwhile the incredible had happened. The French Popular Front Government proposed on August 2nd that all countries should join in agreement of non-intervention in the Spanish Civil War! This policy was accepted with immense relief by Great Britain—as well it might be—and with whoops of joy by the Fascist dictatorships. In the course of time the so-called Committee of Non-Intervention came to include the representatives of twenty-six countries. It met regularly in London and was always dominated by the British.

The British policy was, as usual, both simple and devious. British Conservatives were appalled by revolutionary activities on the side of the Government. Rumours persist that two British bank houses actually financed the insurrection. In any case British commercial interests in Spain were large, and British business men were appalled by the greatly exaggerated picture of 'Spain in anarchy,' skilfully spread by the Fascists. As the inherently pro-Franco London *Times* described the matter in a review of the Spanish situation a year after the outbreak of hostilities:

> 'The considerable sum of foreign investments in Spain, estimated at four hundred million pounds, is an influential factor in Nationalist favour. Nationalist 'reforms' are less feared than the collectivization foreshadowed, and to some extent actually in existence in the territory of the Government at Valencia. This foreign goodwill compensates to an appreciable extent for the lack of gold, which is dire.'

For, as the writer so charmingly stated, on Franco territory, capital and labour do not dispute, strikes would not be tolerated. . . .

But Conservative sympathy for Franco was not the only British reason for welcoming non-intervention. The primary motive is a sincere desire to 'prevent the conflict from spreading'; what the British fear is not foreign intervention but that other Governments should quarrel and eventually fight as a result of it. Since Hitler and Mussolini and Salazar are committed to Franco, and since France favours Valencia, and since Britain simply dare not allow an Italo-German combination to defeat France, the British Cabinet is determined to prevent such a conflict at practically any price. For meanwhile Britain is arming; is growing relatively stronger. Therefore, Britain demands 'more time,' for as Anthony Eden told the House of Commons in July of this year, 'a war postponed may be a war averted.' That this postponement conceivably entails a cold-blooded sacrifice of Spanish democracy no more worries British Conservatives than the memory of their betrayal of Haile Selassie a year ago.

The case with France is different. Leon Blum sympathizes with the Spanish Government. Though British Conservatives fear any sort of 'Popular Front,' the French obviously like it. But France in 1936 was in the midst of financial difficulties and social experiment. The French Conservatives were violently pro-Franco. Blum is a pacifist by conviction and tradition. What if French assistance to Valencia should mean war? What about British support and the Locarno guarantees? The British Admiralty and the British Ambassador found themselves unable to promise France wholehearted British assistance in case support of the Spanish Loyalists should lead to war. Anyway, the Spanish Government needed not only war material, but adequate technicians, which the French were unwilling and unable to supply. The French Radical Party was, as usual, hesitant and divided. And if non-intervention worked, it might actually favour the Spanish Government. Therefore, just as the British Cabinet chose neutrality at any price, so the French chose solidarity with Britain even at cost of important French imperial and strategic interests. And thereby they committed themselves to a policy which furthered the victory of the Fascist Powers and through them of the Spanish Rebels. Once committed they have stuck to it, save for one brief instant in January, when only a stern warning from Paris prevented Berlin from actually landing troops in Spanish Morocco.

Since Fascist dictators consider promises in much the same manner as the late Niccolo Machiavelli, they intervened as much as possible in Spain to the detriment of the Republic. After all, they had respectively got away with the Rhineland re-militarization and the rape of Abyssinia: why should they stop at anything? During August, while Britain and France maintained the embargo, Italy and Germany rushed enough war material to Franco through Portugal to ensure, as they thought, Franco's victory; and early in November, at Berchtesgaden, when Franco's offensive against Madrid had failed, they recognized him diplomatically. When Britain sought to make non-intervention effective by international supervision, the three dictatorships stalled long enough to equip Franco with first-rate war material and a whole Italian army.

When, even after the taking of Malaga and Bilbao the Loyalists still did not collapse and the British pressed hard for the recall of foreign so-called volunteers, the Germans produced a second *Reichstag* fire in the shape of the alleged torpedo attack on the German cruiser *Leipzig*. Badly managed as this comedy was, it served as a pretext for doing away with the system of international supervision which threatened their full liberty of action.

That Franco has not won the war at least three times is due largely to the Soviet Government and the Communist Internationale. In September Russia adhered to the non-intervention agreement and observed it faithfully until it was evident that Italy and Germany and Portugal were cheating wholesale. Whereupon the Soviets began shipping war material to Spain. With Russian aeroplanes and tanks came Russian pilots, technicians, and strategists, among them a general or two. There was never any Russian infantry. But the Communist Internationale was able —thanks to French sympathy—to assemble in Spain the extraordinary group of anti-Fascist volunteers of all nationalities, who became organized as the International Brigades. Frenchmen, Belgians, Germans, Italians, Hungarians, Poles, Dutchmen, thousands of Americans, Englishmen, went to Madrid to fight Fascism. Supported by the Russian Government, these men saved the Spanish Republic. They leavened the young Republican army, they stopped the Moors and Italians, outflew the Germans, died for a conviction. And they began to be ably assisted by the Spanish Communists who, among their countrymen, showed the major capacity for discipline, obedience and perseverance.

Naturally, therefore, the bravest Loyalists flocked to the Communist banner, for at a time like this only a rabbit, a saint, or a super-egoist could refrain from taking sides. Careless of Karl Marx, they affiliated with the group that showed the maximum of discipline and will-power. Communist Party membership rose in eighteen months from about 30,000 to over 300,000, of whom more than 200,000 were actually under arms. Using the influence thus gained, the Communist Internationale came to share responsibility with the Spanish Government, placing their agents with the troops as a substitute for reliable officers. Aware, however, of the realities of the situation they did not greatly seek to implant Communism; they even organized committees to defend the property of the small peasants from anarchists and Trotzky-ites, who pressed for immediate collectivization. They co-operated with Liberals and Socialists in recapturing Catalonia from the anarchists who had virtually 'neutralized' this richest portion of Spain and gave no help in the Civil War. The real responsibility for the spread of 'Red' ideas among the Spaniards lies with the foreign countries, whose refusal to allow the Republic its normal rights drove it into the arms of the friendly Soviets.

Meanwhile in London the Non-Intervention Committee was developing that 'masterly inactivity' which was to 'keep the conflagration from degenerating into a world war.' Italian, German, Portuguese, Russian intervention in Spain was flagrant. War material under the two Spanish flags or the Mexican flag passed with virtual impunity. Dozens of newspaper men reported samples of broken pledges, but in London only the Soviet representative admitted the facts and was hated for doing so. As chairman of the Committee, Anthony Eden saw nothing, heard nothing, knew nothing, admitted nothing—not even what was in British consular reports. When a complete Italian army with its own supply services landed in Cadiz, he simply could not believe his own eyes—and did not. As President Azana accurately described the situation in his speech of

July 18th of this year, non-intervention practically amounted to the following:

The Spanish Government was denied its unquestioned right to buy war material abroad by general agreement among twenty-six countries.

For a certain time the agreement was violated only in favour of the Rebels.

The frontier supervision scheme, finally established, excluded aviation, so that Franco's superiority in the air might be perpetuated.

The application of supervision was postponed until the Insurgents seemed adequately furnished with war material.

Naval supervision was finally established only when the outside world was convinced Franco possessed a decisive advantage.

It was allowed to fall when experience demonstrated Franco's need for still further material if he was to win.

Thus the Spanish Republic was shorn of its rights. Had it been a Great Power it would unquestionably have fought back against Germany, Italy, and Portugal. Instead it submitted to their demands. While, after the *Kamerun* incident, Government ships had to refrain from stopping and searching foreign vessels bearing munitions for Franco, Rebel warships searched or sank Russian cargoes with impunity. Russia was far from the Mediterranean, and Italy, Germany, and conceivably Japan, were more than the Soviets cared to tackle.

As Azaña aptly put it, non-intervention prevented intervention by none but the League of Nations, which had a solemn legal obligation to intervene. Thanks to British and French pressure, a member of the League with a semi-

permanent seat on the Council found the League deaf and
blind to the aggression against it.   Twenty-two years after
the invasion of Belgium, the two great European Democracies treated the League Covenant as a 'scrap of paper.'

Their defence, which was almost a boast, was, they were
keeping the peace.   In the name of peace they conceded
practically everything to Franco and his Allies.   After a
gentle intimation that they really could not permit a modification of the territorial *status quo,* they made no real
effort to protect their own shipping against what was
legally piracy.   At most they continued to press for the
withdrawal from Spanish territory of the foreigners, while
in practice allowing this effort to become an Italo-Germano-
Portuguese attempt to secure for the Rebels so-called
'belligerent right of granting such rights.'   The results
would be to keep the Pyrenees closed while enabling
Franco's warships, secretly assisted by Fascist craft, to keep
all war material from reaching the Loyalists.   This was such
a complete reversal of the original proposal that Russia
refused to accept.   Fearful least the entire smoke-screen be
blown away, the British hastily had the Non-Intervention
Committee adjourned *sine die.*   Today France still keeps
the land frontier closed, but the Spanish sea coasts are open
and ships carrying war material for the Government are
sunk by mysterious submarines.   One might almost think
that, had the *Lusitania* been Spanish, its torpedoing would
have been acclaimed by the British as a meritorious act.

iv. *The Outlook.*

What can come out of the Spanish imbroglio?   Even
a tentative answer to this question demands a preliminary

inquiry into certain things: First, what have thirteen months of Spanish Civil War demonstrated? Second, what is the actual situation in Spain itself? Finally, what, in view of past performance, are the Great Powers likely to do?

1. The greatest result of the Spanish Civil War has been that the chances of a European war have been immensely lessened. Not indeed owing to the Non-Intervention Committee; not through any moral lesson imparted or demonstration of physical horror. Quite the contrary. The Spanish experience has simply shown that the post-War theorists among the military men are wrong: neither the tank nor the areoplane is likely to permit a return to that war of movement wherein alone professional soldiers can find æsthetic satisfaction. Under anything like equal conditions, the defenders still possess the decisive superiority over the attackers which they had at the end of the World War. *Unless and until blasted from his position by some irresistible air or artillery bombardment, the man behind the machine-gun is the lord of the battlefield.* Furthermore, air bombardment does not demoralize a civilian population adequately protected against gas attack. The actual destruction caused by aerial bombs is far less than was assumed. Therefore, the inescapable conclusion that a brief snatch-and-grab attack on an alert adversary is likely to fail. Since the only conceivable aggressors at present are too poor in raw materials, credit and stores, to wage a long conflict, their leaders seem almost bound to refrain from aggression, and general war is postponed.

Specifically, the Spanish experience has revealed other technical facts that reinforce this hypothesis. The new German war material is certainly not superior and hardly seems up to the latest models produced by Germany's democratic neighbours and putative victims. Soviet war material, on the other hand, has turned out to be better than most military experts were ready to admit.

Equally important is—or should be—the demonstration that fifteen years of Italian Fascism have not notably changed the military morale of the Italians. Despite names like *ardita, audace, intrepida, terribile, invincible, implacabile, disperata* and *temeraria* applied to the Italian *Banderas* fighting in Spain, their behaviour has not appreciably differed from that in the World War. Normal, too, was Benito Mussolini's written explanation of the Battle of Guadalajara in which, after alluding casually to a 'crisis of a moral nature,' he concluded that the outcome 'should be called an Italian victory whose exploitation was not permitted by circumstances' but whose dead would be 'avenged.' If the lesson of Guadalajara fails to impress the European general staffs and foreign offices, then their occupants are indeed sunk in lasting trance.

The Spanish experience also tends to show that where all the opponents of Fascist dictatorship unite against it and fight back, they can apparently prevent it from succeeding. It is too often forgotten that neither in Italy nor Germany did the Fascists 'conquer' power, either by armed insurrection or at an election. In both cases they were 'let in,' in Italy by the King, in Germany by President Paul von Hindenburg. The Spanish Pronunciamiento failed even when undertaken by virtually the entire army: without foreign intervention it would have been suppressed in a few weeks.

Favourable to the potential aggressor, on the other hand, is the contemporary demonstration that in free countries the entire population can no longer be rallied to defend incontrovertible national interests. Though German and Italian expansion, even moral, into Spain and Portugal is an unquestioned menace to British and French imperial interests in the Mediterranean, Conservatives in both countries are so eager to see Franco win, so abject in their admiration of Hitler and Mussolini, that they have opposed any reaction that might even indirectly entail a victory of the Spanish so-called 'Reds.'

The Spanish experience reveals something else, namely, that with the new technique of mixing truth, half truth, falsehood, denial and counter-charge, world public opinion can be so manipulated that the situation in a great country can be successfully misrepresented. It had been assumed that in an age of radio and telephone everything must be open and above board. And instead, not only have the Governments (including the democracies) reverted to secret diplomacy, but they have increased the smoke-screen by manipulation to the point where the most blatant facts can be rendered uncertain in the minds of millions. This possibility of deceiving the masses is unquestionably a weapon in the hands of Governments which it was never intended they should have.

2. What is the situation in Spain after thirteen months of fighting?

General Francisco Franco and his foreign Allies hold slightly more than half the territory, with something less than half the population. They control a large share of the mineral wealth, but a small part of the national industry. They have no gold, but are lavishly helped by Germany and Italy, and have managed to maintain credits elsewhere. They possess the support of all big business men whose chief bogey is Bolshevism and who fail to recognize this in its Fascist form. The so-called stamped or Franco peseta is quoted in London at two or three times the value of Government money, thus showing how the world financiers estimate the relative chances of the two groups. Franco's emissaries abroad are on the whole more favourably received than Valencia's.

The population in Rebel territory was immediately intimidated by wholesale terror, and lives under military law. There is no pretence about democracy or freedom of speech. The ultra-Fascist element which took care of the 'social cleansing' behind the lines, while leaving most of the fighting to the Moors, white and black, to regular Spanish soldiers and to Requetés from Northern Spain, has been somewhat subdued. There is a certain amount of shaking down the ungrateful rich in order to get money and talk of 'social reforms' along Italian or German lines. Franco himself explained in a decree of October 3, 1936, that in the Spain he hopes to dominate 'there will be no suffrage, but the country will be reorganized on ideally Spanish lines,' apparently meaning the re-establishment of the supremacy of the Church, the landowners and the business magnates, and conceivably the monarchy, although many suspect that after his taste of power, Franco will be more likely to follow the inimitable Horthy in Hungary and establish himself as a more or less permanent Regent with monarchical privileges.

Franco's fleet is good, but his army is not entirely satisfactory to him. There is no longer much enthusiasm to join it on the part of Spaniards. Of its 350,000 odd members, the Spanish contingent cannot number over 200,000. The rest are Italians, Germans, Moors and a sparse sprinkling of foreign volunteers from other countries.

Thanks to Italy, Germany and Portugal, the army is better equipped than that of the Loyalists; it is amply supplied with artillery, machine-guns and ammunition, and maintains superiority in tanks and in the air. Its officer corps is reasonably good, and its staff work shows German influence. But its component national elements do not relish each other's presence. As the American correspondent A. R. Knickerbocker wrote:

'The Germans in Spain despise the Italians and detest the Spaniards. The Italians hate the Germans and loathe the Spaniards. The Spaniards abhor both Italians and Germans, and everybody is sick of war' (*The New York Journal*, May 1, 1937).

Add to this the gifficulty of recruiting Moors equal to the superb savages Franco first brought from Morocco and the picture is complete.

Utterly different is the situation in Loyalist territory. Administration, transport, industrial conditions, war preparations were worse than non-existent. The Valencia authorities have had a terrific fight to re-acquire authority from the labour committees, who seized power and arms and cared more for keeping both than for carrying on an unpleasant Civil War in districts remote from the town pump. The army had to be organized from scratch, with the assistance of Russians, Frenchmen and other foreigners. Only gradually were the industries indispensable to the conduct of war brought under some sort of control and production re-established. Liberals, socialists of two or three sorts, communists, Trotzky-ites and anarchists quarrelled among themselves and strove for power.

Catalonia, the richest and most populous province, with 20 per cent of agricultural production and 25 per cent of industry, fell into the hands of anarchist committees who murdered and stole, seized and hid away valuable war material, interrupted important communications with France, and were almost useless at the front even when they consented to pass a brief vacation in the lines. Yet without Catalonia the Civil War could not be won by the Loyalists.

Slowly, in typical Spanish fashion, the Government managed to re-establish its authority, dominate Catalonia, restore order and legality, subjugate the various factions, organize a vast militia and transform it gradually into an army, obtain supplies, some support and even volunteers abroad. Today this work is reasonably well advanced. Some months from now it will begin to show fruits on a large scale.

The Loyalist army today consists of 400,000 or 500,000 men, of whom not more than 25,000 are foreigners. Of these masses, hardly over 100,000 are properly trained and equipped. There is a lasting shortage of munitions, artillery and aeroplanes. But the army is distinctly on the upgrade and could already dispense with foreign volunteers altogether save on the staffs, where Russians and a few Frenchmen remain of great value.

The navy, on the other hand, has never recovered from the initial demoralization that followed the murder of the Fascist officers by the crews in order to prevent the former from delivering the ships to Franco. Here, too, foreign help is indispensable if anything is to be done.

In theory, the regime is Republican bourgeois under the old Constitution; in practice 'war socialist' under Government supervision. As President Azana stated:

'There is no danger of waking up one morning and finding Communism ruling the country. My purpose is to prevent the accumulation of great wealth by a few individuals while many suffer from hunger and poverty.'

The millions of bourgeois who support the Republic do so in the belief that although victory is bound to leave some Socialism behind, small property will be protected. There seems no ground for the belief that foreign property owners will be despoiled. Freedom of religion will be respected. Already one convent has been reopened at Valencia. There is no evidence of any permanent Russian influence.

Both sides are equally sincere. Therefore, however terrible the Civil War may seem to foreigners, to Spaniards in Spain it is not a 'tragedy.' To die for a cause you consider great is not tragic. To the Rebels, convinced that God, tradition, order and interest are on their side, the revolt is legitimate and holy. To the Republicans it provides a sad but glorious opportunity for finally enfranchising Spain from medieval obscurantism, military tyranny, economic serfdom and national ignominy. But though the passion is equal on both sides, there is not the slightest doubt but that the larger mass of Spaniards prefers a 'pink' Republic to the theocratic Fascism offered by Franco.

3. What may be expected of the Great Powers? Portugal is at most an important pawn. Salazar must do what his big confederates dictate, though he knows well that after such acts as delivering refugees from Badajoz back into the hands of their Rebel executioners he can expect short shrift from a victorious Spanish Republic.

Italy and Germany have linked themselves by the Pact of Berchtesgaden to work together in Spain, in Austria, in matters pertaining to Locarno and 'against Communism,' meaning against Soviet Russia. To appraise their movements one must consider them separately as ambitious Great Powers, to which Spanish intervention is but one step in a glorious series; as bankrupt nationalistic States; and as the twin pillars of Fascist doctrine. Let us consider Italy first.

Italy is seeking to found an empire on a shoe-string. Its strategic position within the Mediterranean, with most of its important towns vulnerable to naval attack, is considered even by German theorists as disastrous. The Powers that control the Western Mediterranean control Italy, which must either submit to them or seek to break their grip. By controlling Spain Italy can emancipate itself from France and Britain. Even possession of the Balearic Islands goes some distance along this line. The Spanish Civil War is a heaven-sent opportunity to do this without a major war, which Italy is not morally or materially in a position to win. With part of his army in Ethiopia, the more men Mussolini sends to Spain the worse his position strategically becomes. But after his victory over the League he is convinced, first, that British and French democracies are afraid to fight; second, that Conservatives in both countries fear to defeat him lest his regime develop into some more open form of Collectivism. Ambition drives him on and fear, for at any point his adversaries may tire of blackmail and decide to crush him. In his heart he knows that to fight with Germany as ally would be the end of Italian independence. Thus big words lead to bigger words, intervention in Spain to further intervention. If it goes far enough, Franco's collapse might mean Mussolini's, and the reversion of Italy to its normal political dimensions.

As a bankrupt State Italy would like to make sure of

certain metallic supplies—mercury, copper and iron—at advantageous conditions. It cannot afford to lose the war material already shipped to Spain. It can hardly support its present military expenses. In the long run, Mussolini knows that in the armament race with the rich democracies neither Italy nor its German ally can long stand the present pace. Therefore, the Spanish intervention must be brought to fruition quickly.

Germany as a 'dynamic' Great Power is primarily interested in weakening France, particularly the France of the Popular Front. For this purpose any Spain will do, sufficiently strong and hostile to menace the French communications with the North African source of man power. It can also be achieved by obtaining influence in the Canaries and the Spanish West African Rio de Oro. Once France is weakened, Germany can force the restitution of colonies or the admission of its right to expand in Austria, Czechoslovakia and Poland.

As a pauper State, which has nonetheless, according to the London *Banker*, spent no less than twelve billion dollars in four years for re-armament, but which is now being outdistanced by Britain and France, Germany must either moderate its ambition, which is unthinkable, or obtain British support, or continue to intimidate the pacific democracies, conceivably acquiring valuable naval bases in the process. But the German army cannot face an immediate war and has far too little trust in Italy to continue sacrificing valuable war material for any Spanish stake. For the German second four-year plan of economic self-sufficiency is a failure, and from month to month internal economic pressure grows.

Ideologically Germany and Italy are indivisible. As

somebody said, a Fascist despotism resembles a bicycle that must continue at a good speed or fall. Fascism is a world-wide movement directed against the Classical-Christian-Renaissance tradition out of which came modern science, modern art, modern self-government, personal liberty and a beginning of world-organizations. Mussolini himself said of the democracies:

'The struggle between two worlds can permit no compromise. Either their ideas or ours. Either their State or ours.'

In other words, there can be no hope of a live-and-let-live relationship between totalitarian Fascism and liberal democracy. A Fascist victory in Spain is a victory over Britain, France, the United States and the League of Nations, far more, in my opinion, than over the Soviets. For several years Fascism has been gaining and, as a British newspaper man recently wrote, 'We are seeing all over Europe the lights that shine in the faces of free men and women go out one by one.' For Fascism it is indispensable that these lights go out in Spain. Therefore, in the name of the preservation and justification of their system, Germany and Italy will go as far as they dare and can to assure the victory of Franco, whom they expect to dominate and direct after he comes to power. Although both States are fundamentally weak, they can go on as long as they meet no serious resistance.

The French Republic, uneasy, vaguely aware of the Fascist threats, generally desirous of a victory for the Spanish Republic, but pacifist, socially divided, dependent upon Great Britain, is too frightened to do more for that Republic than connive at the passage of some contraband war material. Only if encouraged by Great Britain would

France conceivably compel by threat of force Germany and Italy to withdraw from Spain and withdraw the threat on France's vital lines of communication.

Does anybody believe the British people give this encouragement? More pacifist than the French, more socially divided, fearful of something called Bolshevism in Russia but praised as order in Fascist countries, the British are yielding one vital position after another to weaker opponents, consoling themselves with the hope that Spanish xenophobia will be too strong for Italy or Germany to remain dominant in the Peninsula. Truly Britain is re-arming on a giant scale, but it was not for lack of resources that Rome fell. There is little evidence that the British will make use of the re-acquired power. Certainly not in defence of anything so vague as world democracy or collective security, which is probably inseparable from it. For, incredible as it is, the mass of Britishers have never realized that Fascism is something new and infinitely dangerous to their own sort of life. Once they fought Napoleon for years as a foreign tyrant; today, hypnotized by the supposed 'Bolshevik danger,' they remain inert in face of something far worse because capable of spreading to Britain. In fact, they seem distinctly flattered by the alternate abuse and flattery which they receive from Germany and Italy, and their diplomacy toys with the notion of 'separating the two dangers.'

Only Soviet Russia will continue to oppose the Fascists in Spain. But unobtrusively, indirectly, unofficially as heretofore. Doubtless many Russians hope that a Franco victory will eventually mean a Communist Spain. But although Russia realizes the inherent weakness of the Fascist States, it dare not come to an open break with them over a hypothetical stake so remote from Moscow. The Soviets have no intention of attacking anybody.

Secure in its isolation, its heart overflowing with sympathy for the Spanish Republic, the United States of America will continue to proffer good advice, while refusing to furnish fellow-Republicans with that vital war material that could save their existence.

v. *The Possible Consequences.*

This being the situation, what hope is there for the Spanish Republic? Just a fighting chance, if the non-intervention fiction be maintained. What Italy and Germany most fear is the opening of France to free trade, and transit in arms. But even as matters are, even if Spain be again bulldozed into renouncing its rights as a League Member, it is not at all certain that Franco will win. How long *can* Italy and *will* Germany continue to invest their war material in what may prove a waste? The Russians will continue so long as the Republic has a chance. Franco must score a decisive success before snow again falls on the mountains of Castille, or be prepared next spring to face a large, well-trained and even better equipped Loyalist army—unless, that is, Britain and France meanwhile consent to allow a blockade of the Loyalist coasts! Without non-intervention the Loyalists, in my opinion, would have better than an even chance. It is therefore a sort of race between the Republic's capacity for putting a real army into the field and the ability of Franco's Allies to win a quick victory for him—for by himself he has not even a remote possibility of success. Therefore he can never consent to the departure of his foreign Allies. So the war will go on to some sort of decision. Personally, I do not believe in the practicability of any sort of mediation or compromise.

And if Franco wins? Then we shall see whether or not the Western democracies still possess the courage to live, without which they, and their system with them, are doomed. Peace cannot be bought by cowardly concessions, and democracy must again become fervent, or it will cease to be.

If, on the other hand, the Republic wins, then Fascism has received a terrific blow, Britain and French national interests are safe, the chances of further aggression elsewhere are greatly minimized and, for the first time since the Japanese seizure of Manchuria, there will be an opportunity for a second effort towards world-organization and stability.

CHAPTER IV

THE BREAKDOWN OF THE SYSTEM OF COLLECTIVE SECURITY

by

DR. G. P. GOOCH

TODAY we no longer ask the question: Has the collective system broken down? We take the lamentable fact as our starting-point and proceed to investigate its causes. I should like, however, to suggest a correction in the title of my address. A system can only collapse when it has been a reality. Collective security has never functioned. Let us speak therefore of the breakdown of a plan, the disappointment of a hope. The noble conception of an organized, interdependent, co-operating world, based on the reign of law, has not failed, for it has never been tried. Two decades after the Covenant began to take shape the European situation has been compared by Mr. Chamberlain to the danger of the high mountains, where a loud voice can start an avalanche.

i. *Survival of the Sovereign State.*

Let us pass in review some of the reasons for our sorry plight. Firstly, there is the evil tradition of the Sovereign State, under which we have all lived for the last four centuries. The finest minds of the Middle Ages thought in terms of a *Respublica Christiana*, which, despite its geographical and theological limitations, recognized at any rate that the national unit was part of a larger organic whole. With the dawn of a new age, inaugurated by the Renaissance and the Reformation, by Machiavelli and Copernicus, by Columbus and Vasco da Gama, the horizon widened but the conception of community waned. The self-sufficing State, bound by no allegiance, legal or moral, to anything outside or above itself, gave the more advanced countries a measure of internal order to which the Middle Ages never attained. But a rising standard of organization at home was not accompanied by a corresponding improvement in the relations of States. Independence, not interdependence, was the watchword. War was not only the *ultima ratio* but the universally accepted instrument of national policy. Diplomacy without armaments, declared Frederick the Great, was like music without instruments.

A few prophets like Penn, Saint Pierre and Kant pointed out a better way. Sporadic attempts were made during the nineteenth century—the Holy Alliance, the system of Conferences, the Concert of Europe in the Eastern Question, the growth of arbitration, the creation of the Hague Court—to hold mankind together. Yet the outworn fetish of the Sovereign State survived with little modification into the twentieth century, and the cause of the World War, as Lowes Dickinson's well-known work explained, was the European Anarchy. Shaken in our complacency by the greatest catastrophe in history, we challenged its claims and showed signs of setting out on another path. But man needs time to learn his lessons, and the vast confusion, material and spiritual, which followed the War has driven us backward instead of forward. The unity of mankind, the federation of the world, remains a beautiful dream.

c*

ii. *Imperfections of the Peace Settlement.*

The second cause of the failure of the plan of collective
security was the radical imperfection of the Peace Settlement. Mr Keynes spoke of the Treaty of Versailles as a
Carthaginian peace. Whether or no we accept his pic-
turesque adjective, it is a commonplace today that one of
the great opportunities of modern history was lost. 'All
power corrupts,' declared Acton in a memorable aphorism,
'and absolute power corrupts absolutely.' The victorious
Allies in 1918–19 possessed absolute power. They proved
themselves unworthy of it by making precisely the same
sort of peace as Germany, judging by the Treaty of Brest-
Litovsk, would have forced down our throats had she won
the War. A dictated settlement, reached without oral discussion and framed within sight of the devastated regions
of France, was bound to prove a rickety foundation for a
new international order. The priest of Nemi, in the old
legend, had slain his predecessor, and it was fated that he
too should be slain. What had been won by the sword
could only be held by the sword. Dragon's teeth were
sown and have come up as armed men. That the loser
pays is the accepted rule of the gamble of war. Alsace-
Lorraine, 'the challenge-cup of Europe,' passed back to
France, and North Schleswig to Denmark. But the
severity of the punishment surpassed all expectations,
particularly in the extent of territory given to the new
Poland, the confiscation of the whole colonial empire, the
principle on which the payment of reparations was fixed,
and the imputation of sole responsibility for the conflict.
The cooler heads, who were found chiefly in the British
and American Delegations, were overborne by the French

triumvirate, Clemenceau, Poincaré and Foch, who could not see beyond the end of their noses.

iii. *Incompleteness of the League.*

The third cause of our present discontents was the incompleteness of the League which began its formal existence in January 1920. Russia's abstention was regrettable but not actually disastrous. It is a tragic paradox that the chief architect was unable to lead his country into the stately edifice which he described as the only hope for the world. It is a common error to believe that the Senate refused to enter the League. It was quite ready to do so subject to the Lodge reservations, which Wilson refused to accept. Colonel House has expressed his belief that, if he had remained *persona grata* at the White House, he could have persuaded the President to swallow the dose, unnecessary and undesirable though it was. The magnitude of the loss to Europe and the world was only gradually recognized as the fatal predominance of France in the post-War years was emphasized. America had helped to defeat Germany, yet in some measure she stood apart. She asked neither territory nor indemnities. Her moderating influence was sorely missed on the Reparation Commission and elsewhere. Without her the League might well seem to the defeated countries, to quote the pungent formula of Sir Ian Hamilton, a committee of conquerors.

Only less disastrous to the stabilization of Europe was the absence of Germany. America stayed out by her own will. Germany was excluded by the decision of the Allies. It would no doubt have been inexpressibly painful to the representatives of England, France and Belgium to sit at the same table with their terrible foe while the wounds of war were fresh. But a little more magnanimity, a little more imagination, a little more common sense, in the hour of victory would have shaped a very different world from that on which we look out today. France rose from the dust after her defeat in 1870, and Germany was certain to do the same.

The resilience of a great nation is amazing. Its soul is indestructible and its body quickly recovers. In what mood would Germany be when her strength returned? I remember a question being addressed to Norman Angell at a meeting during the War: What would our formidable enemy be like, what would she do, when the struggle was over? That would mainly depend on how she was treated, was his reply. He was a true prophet. We are paying the penalty of our short-sightedness. The French refused to admit the Germans when the League was launched. They refused again when Mr Lloyd George informally proposed it in 1922. 'Pas encore!' said President Millerand. Another lost opportunity! Of the seven Great Powers, only four were members of the League. It was like a man starting out on a long walk with a lame leg.

iv. *French Policy*, 1918–24.

A fourth cause of the failure to create a system of security was the policy of France from the end of the War till the victory of the Left in the elections of 1924. The Treaty of Versailles was bad enough, but the spirit in which it was carried out was even worse. The *Bloc National,* represented by Poincaré and Millerand, committed exactly the same mistake as victorious Germany after 1871. In both cases the defeated nation was made to drink the cup of humiliation to the dregs. The stationing of black troops in the Rhineland, though not intended as a provocation, was passionately resented in Germany, where France's tolerant attitude to coloured people was unknown. Far worse was the encouragement of separatist movements in the Rhineland and Bavaria by making use of the scum of the population. Worst of all was the invasion of the Ruhr in 1923, on the pretext that reparation payments were in arrears. As an economic measure it was a failure, as a fresh revelation of France's implacable hostility a psychological blunder of the first magnitude. It was met by passive resistance, the miners and railwaymen of Germany's Black Country refusing to work for the invader. The maintenance of the population in idleness sent the mark, already worth only a fraction of its pre-War value, tumbling into the bottomless abyss, carrying with it the investments and savings of one of the thriftiest peoples on earth.

Europe breathed a sigh of relief when the *Bloc National* was succeeded in May 1924 by Herriot, the Liberal leader. Briand, who dominated French foreign policy in the following years, announced in a famous phrase that they must all learn to talk European, and reassured the mothers of France by the pledge: 'Tant que je serai là il n'y aura pas de guerre.' The troops were withdrawn from the Ruhr, the Dawes Scheme reduced the extravagant reparation claims of the Allies to a more manageable proposition, the Locarno Treaty was made, Germany entered the League, the Kellogg Pact was signed, and in June 1930, five years before the treaty limit, the last soldiers of the Army of Occupation marched out of the Rhineland. The first six years after the War, 1918–24, were as bad as they could be. The second six years, 1924-30, the era in which Stresemann, Briand and Chamberlain worked in harmony, brought hope back into the world. We can now see that it was a false dawn. The foundations were insecure. The Thoiry vision of Franco-German reconciliation and co-operation remained a dream. Locarno came too late and was not followed up. The wounds of war had not yet healed.

v. *Failure to Agree on Armaments.*

A fifth cause of our failure to rebuild Europe was the mishandling of the problem of armaments by the victorious Powers. It was a triumph of common sense when the Washington Naval Treaty of 1922 rationed the battleships of Great Britain, the United States, Japan, France and Italy. But nothing was done to lift the burden on land. There was much to be said for the limitation of Germany's armaments in the Treaty of Versailles if her victors had proceeded to abandon the categories which she was forbidden to possess. This was never seriously considered, despite the moral obligation on all members of the League under Article 8 of the Covenant. The terrible memories of the War rendered it impossible to contemplate equality of status with the defeated foe. Thus another opportunity was thrown away. Since the Allies declined to scale down their armaments to the German level, Germany was certain to climb towards theirs as soon as she felt strong enough to do so with impunity.

The Disarmament Conference which opened at Geneva in February 1932 had taken years to prepare, and it met too late. Even the chance of a limited agreement was lost owing to the lack of a strong lead at the outset by a Great

Power, corresponding to the vigorous American initiative at the Washington Naval Conference. Each country was virtuously ready for reductions in categories which were not of vital importance to itself, but stood out for those which it needed most. Thus Great Britain longed for the abolition of the submarine, which nearly starved us in 1917, while she clung to the capital ship. Italy professed her readiness to accept the lowest standard acceptable to others, and President Hoover, after the Conference had been at work for several months, proposed a clean cut of one-third over the whole field. The statesmen failed to stand up against the experts, who could always supply cogent reasons for refusing this limitation or that. The longer the discussion, the more distant seemed the goal. When the Conference adjourned for the summer holidays in 1932, it was clear that it had failed. In the autumn Germany retired, but was brought back by a promise of equality of status in the matter of armaments within a system of general security. Such a system proved unattainable, and a year later Hitler's Germany withdrew not only from the Conference but from the League itself. His subsequent offer to accept an army limit lower than France was rejected by Barthou, the political heir of Poincaré, in the spring of 1934. Another tragic blunder! Since that moment Germany has been re-arming at feverish speed, and Europe is back again in its pre-War mood when everyone was afraid of Berlin. Our own colossal re-armament programme is the measure of our alarm.

vi. *The Economic Slump.*

A sixth cause of our troubles was the great slump which began with the bursting of the speculation bubble in New

York at the close of 1929. The blizzard crossed the
Atlantic and fell on Europe with pitiless fury in 1930. To
Germany it brought not only economic suffering but
political revolution. For if the Treaty of Versailles and
French policy down to 1924 gave Hitler a start, his ship
was floated into harbour by the exasperation of masses of
Germans at the renewal of their troubles. The figures of
the Reichstag elections of 1924, 1928 and 1930 tell their
own tale. The Nazis secured fewer seats and fewer votes
in 1928 than in 1924, whereas in 1930 their representation
jumped up from 12 to 107. Henceforth Brüning fought
a losing battle, while Hitler rapidly advanced, scattering
denunciations, threats and promises on his way. There is
no more poignant tragedy in post-War history than the
fact that the mistakes of the victorious Allies have done far
more than his own eloquence to lift the Nazi dictator into
the saddle. It is the old story of the Sibylline books.
What we refused to Rathenau, Stresemann and Brüning,
in a word to Weimar Germany, we have been forced or may
be forced to concede to a leader whose gospel of violence and
racial intolerance is stridently proclaimed in *Mein Kampf*.

vii. *Failures to Stop Aggression.*

If the great slump descended on us from beyond the
Atlantic, the first staggering blow at the system of collective
security came from the Far East. Let us reckon the rape of
Manchuria in 1931 as the seventh item in our list of regrets.
In building an empire by force Japan is merely following
in the footsteps of other Powers, including ourselves. The
novelty was the fact that she deliberately broke three very
recent treaties—the Covenant of the League, the Nine

Power Treaty of Washington of 1922, and the Kellogg Pact renouncing war as an instrument of national policy. That China exerted no effective control over her northern provinces could not alter the fact that in international law Manchuria was her property, as it had been for centuries.

The builders of the League were well aware that the real test of the system of collective security would come if and when a Great Power aggressed. Little States had been brought to heel without much difficulty. But what could the League do against a powerful offender at the other end of the world, armed to the teeth, and flushed by the memory of recent victories on land and sea? It possessed neither troops, ships nor aeroplanes. If economic sanctions were applied, Japan might retaliate. However improbable such a contingency, it had to be borne in mind. Which of the Powers, large or small, were willing to face the risk? None, as it turned out. The Lytton Commission of Inquiry was sent out and did its work with admirable thoroughness. On the basis of its report the action of Japan was unanimously denounced by the members of the League, and it was decided to refuse recognition to the puppet State of Manchukuo, the child of sin. So far, so good. But that was all. Mr Stimson's book shows that he was willing to go a little further than Sir John Simon, yet the Washington Government never suggested the application of economic sanctions. Japan had chosen her time well. The world was in the grip of the great slump, and no State had stomach for a fight. There were many reasons or excuses for doing nothing. Yet the fact remains that the successful aggression of Japan struck a felon blow at the League and invited imitation of her lawless action by other dissatisfied States.

As an eighth cause of the failure of collective security

may be reckoned the inability of the League, or of any other mediator, to prevent or to stop the Chaco war. For three years Bolivia and Paraguay bled each other white in the dark forests of South America, and only mutual exhaustion brought the conflict to an end. The impotence of the League, to which both belligerents belonged, was regrettable enough. But what are we to say of the countries or rather of the firms who, with the consent of their Governments, supplied the combatants with the arms they could not manufacture themselves? Never before had the evils of the private manufacture of munitions been brought so vividly before our eyes. If the vendors of lethal weapons, living as they are bound to do on any orders they can get, do not make our wars, they profit by their outbreak and prolong the conflict.

A ninth cause of trouble is perhaps the most heart-breaking of all. General de Bono has revealed in his recent book how Mussolini decided in 1933 to conquer Abyssinia. The Walwal incident, which for propaganda purposes was taken as the starting-point, only occurred at the end of 1934, and the first troops were despatched in February 1935. It was thus a case of calculated aggression, carried through with a cynical disregard of treaty obligations. While Japan broke three solemn pacts, Italy broke four. By the agreement of 1906 she pledged herself to consult England and France in relation to Abyssinia. Under Article 10 of the Covenant she undertook to respect the integrity and independence of her fellow-members of the League. By the Kellogg Pact she renounced war as an instrument of national policy. By her treaty with Abyssinia in 1928 she agreed that disputes should be settled by peaceful methods alone.

How did the League respond to this daring challenge? It did more than in the case of Manchuria, but it intervened too late. Indeed the battle was lost before it raised its voice. For in January 1935 Laval visited Mussolini and liquidated differences which had kept France and Italy on bad terms ever since the War. Did he also consent to the invasion of Abyssinia then about to begin? He denies it. Only the economic aspect of the Abyssinian question, he assures us, was discussed. In the absence of precise information we can only guess. Whatever may have been said, Mussolini's subsequent course suggests that he anticipated no opposition on the part of France. His inquiry in London shortly after as to our interests in Abyssinia was referred to an inter-departmental Committee, which took months to report. Meanwhile, though the British and French Premiers met the Duce at Stressa in May and formed the so-called Stressa front, Abyssinia, we were told, was not discussed, though men and munitions were pouring through the Suez Canal, and it was generally anticipated that the attack would begin at the close of the summer rains.

The British Government's well-meant offer to Abyssinia of the Port of Zeila in British Somaliland as a lever to procure Abyssinian concessions to Italy failed as completely as the efforts in Paris and Geneva to produce an acceptable compromise. When the Assembly met in September it seemed as if nothing could be done. All the more sensational was the trumpet-call of Sir Samuel Hoare on September 11, summoning the world to stand by the principle of collective security and defining England's policy as that of steady and collective resistance to unprovoked aggression. The world-wide impression made by the speech was enhanced by his suggestion of an inquiry into the problem of access to raw materials as one of the leading causes of discontent and insecurity. For a moment it seemed as if the League had come to life and was about to discharge its lofty function as the guardian of righteousness and peace.

Like the sunshine of Locarno, it was a false dawn. A month after the Hoare declaration Italian troops crossed the Abyssinian frontier. The League decided, in accordance with its duty under Article 16, to impose economic sanctions, or, to express it more exactly, to withhold supplies to the aggressor. A first list of articles was drawn up, in which oil, the most important of all, was conspicuous by its absence. For Mussolini declared that, while Italy would bear the minor deprivations with fortitude, the refusal of the oil needed for his lorries and aeroplanes was a military measure and would be answered by war. When the burglar showed his teeth the policemen ran away. The final humiliation, for which Geneva was not responsible, was the Hoare-Laval scheme of partition hurriedly launched at Paris at the end of 1935, and speedily buried amid the execrations of the British people. Yet the mischief was done. Mussolini had triumphed. He had never been really alarmed. For he knew that the France of Laval would not push things to extremity, and that without French co-operation England would not dream of closing the Suez Canal.

Aided by unlimited supplies of oil and poison gas, and stung in her national pride by the moral indignity of sanctions, Italy defeated her foe, contrary to general expectations, before the summer rains of 1936. So complete was the humiliation of the League that many people who had hitherto supported Article 16 as an essential factor in a system of collective security now advocated its elimination and the transformation of the League into a purely consultative body. Never in the sixteen years of its life had its prestige fallen so low as in the summer of 1936, when the Emperor fled from his country and Italian troops marched into Addis Ababa. It seemed as if the Fascist Empire had been founded on the ruins of the League. Yet, when we speak of the failure of that institution, we merely mean the refusal of its more powerful members to carry out their obligations.

How little the League seemed to count in the life of the world was revealed anew when civil war broke out in Spain in July 1936. Here is the tenth of our regrets. It was no part of its duty to intervene in internal affairs of one of its members, so long as the conflict was of a purely domestic character. But when Italian troops in their thousands joined the Rebels and invaded Spain and the Balearic isles, the conflict became a European issue. For under an authoritarian regime there are no 'volunteers.' Not a man, not a gun, not a bombing aeroplane, could have left Italy without the orders of the Dictator. The European aspect of the struggle was intensified when volunteers from many countries, enrolled in the International Brigade, arrived in the autumn and saved Madrid at the eleventh hour. On more than one occasion the Spanish Government laid its case before the League. But the will to attempt mediation was lacking. The world's verdict on Manchuria and Abyssinia was almost unanimous. In regard to Spain opinion on the merits of the contending parties is so deeply divided that the fatalistic attitude has been adopted of letting the warring parties and their foreign backers blow each other to pieces, and trusting to the so-called

Non-Intervention Committee in London to avert the spread of the conflagration.

viii. *Unwillingness for Peaceful Change.*

The story of the breakdown of the plan of collective security is above all a record of lost opportunities. I have left to the last the neglect to employ Article 19 of the Covenant. Let us call it the eleventh of our laments. President Wilson knew enough of history and human nature to be aware that the world does not stand still, that treaties do not last for ever. As Bismarck used to say, every agreement contains an unwritten article that it only remains valid *rebus sic stantibus.* The permission to members of the League to suggest the revision of treaties was an organic part of a scheme which came into being at the same time as a number of treaties imposed by the victors on their prostrate foes. Here was the oil to make the wheels revolve without dangerous friction, the safety-valve to prevent explosions, the invitation to statesmen to deal with grievances before they festered into war.

Why this admirable Article has never been applied is clear enough. Japan and Italy knew that they would not get Manchuria and Abyssinia by asking for them, for they had no shadow of legal or moral claim. But supposing that an arguable request for territorial revision were to be made, that Germany, for instance, pleaded the unfairness of possessing no colonial empire. The League could only appoint a commission to report, and, if so minded, recommend the adoption of its plan. The final decision would remain with the country which was asked to make the sacrifice. And where is such a country to be found?

Small concessions would fail to satisfy, and large concessions are at present ruled out by public opinion. The instinct to hold what we have got, whether by war or inheritance, is very strong. When has a State given up anything except as part of a deal? The gift of the Ionian Isles to Greece by the Palmerston Ministry stands out as a solitary example of unforced generosity. And while the shadow of another world war hangs over us, how can we avoid pondering the strategic value of any territory which comes up for consideration? How can we forget the magnificent opportunities offered by Tanganyika, for instance, as a basis for submarine and aerial attack, to say nothing of the formidable native army which Germany could train?

It is a commonplace that the issue of peace or war turns on the question of the possibility of peaceful change in the next few years. Of the seven Great Powers in the world, four (Great Britain, France, Russia and the United States) are absolutely satisfied with their share of the earth's surface. They are no better than the rest, but they have had the luck of the deal. The other three, Japan, Italy and Germany, are dissatisfied, though Abyssinia will doubtless still the pangs of hunger for a time. From their own point of view the claim of these countries to territorial redistribution is very strong, and even outsiders can visualize their emotions. That the British Empire embraces a quarter of the earth's surface seems to most of its citizens the most natural and rational thing in the world. To others it appears an indefensible anomaly. How readjustments should be made, and who should make them; how far economic internationalism or League control might diminish the craving for colonial territory; what conditions should be imposed if native populations change their masters; what the beneficiary should give, for instance in the field of disarmament, in return for value received—these and similar questions are outside the scope of my address. My modest task has been to record some of the graver mistakes of recent years. How to retrace our steps when we realize that we have taken a wrong turning, how to struggle out of the dark forest into the light of day, is infinitely more difficult. All that I can say with complete assurance is that a system of collective security will only become a living reality when all the Great Powers of the world are moderately contented with their lot.

CHAPTER V

WORLD CO-OPERATION IN HEALTH

by
MELVILLE D. MACKENZIE, M.D.
Member of the Health Section of the League of Nations Secretariat
Formerly Acting Director of the Singapore Epidemiological Bureau

i. *Introduction : the Necessity for International Collaboration in Medicine.*

I DO not propose, in this paper, simply to speak of the value of international collaboration in medical work as this is a self-evident proposition. I intend rather to catalogue briefly some of the aspects of the medical work upon which the Health Organization of the League of Nations is engaged. My object in doing so is two-fold. In the first place it will enable you to realize the number of lines along which international collaboration in medicine has already achieved results ; and secondly, suggest to your imagination the almost limitless scope and possibilities for the future. Medicine is, as a fundamental necessity of humanity, of wider application than the League itself, and the existence of the Health organization of the League may be looked upon simply as an instance of the greatest of sciences lending its help in the cause of peace. But it is more than this. It is a mutual alliance—a symbiosis— from which both parties obtain advantages. What does the League gain ? In the first place international medical work illustrates to the whole world, in terms that no political party can gainsay, the profits of the collaboration between countries. As in the case of thought, ideals, music and the arts, we are dealing, in the case of disease, with an entity which can know no political frontiers. Secondly, medicine demonstrates the individual responsibility of each country, not only as a unit itself, but as a member of a community of countries—that is, with international as well as with national responsibilities. A single plague rat arriving on a ship from an infected country and starting a plague epidemic in a healthy country brings home vividly to the Governments concerned the interdependence of one country on the precautions taken by its neighbour. There can be no policy of 'splendid isolation' from plague rats, yellow fever, mosquitoes, or cholera-infected water. Thirdly, for the League, medicine illustrates the value to all Governments of a neutral liaison officer, in this case medical, but suggesting the application of the method to wider fields.

When cholera, for instance, sweeps across Asia, administrations are quick to realize the value of some centre—not under any Government—where information as to the spread of the disease can be collected, where details as to the steps being taken to control the disease in each country are procurable, and where medical officers are available who can at any time visit the various focuses of the disease. These officers, not belonging to any Government or any political party, are welcomed where difficulties would be experienced by the visit of a national representative.

All this for the League. What has medicine gained?

For the first time in the history of humanity the Covenant of the League, and the consequent formation of the Health Organization, offered a machine for the co-ordination of research work in every branch of medicine in all nations. It offered for the first time the opportunity of comparing the results—successful or otherwise—of medical administrative steps in various countries. It is now possible to pool experience in the laboratory, by the bedside, and in the field, for the advancement of medicine and the benefit of humanity. It is true that, prior to the formation of the Health Organization of the League international, collaboration existed, but only in connexion with the extremely limited field of legislation against five diseases—yellow fever, cholera, plague, smallpox and typhus fever. Except in this very restricted domain, the whole of the possibilities of international collaboration in medicine were unexplored. It was natural, therefore, that in its earliest stages much of the work of the Health Organization should be exploratory in character. International medicine stood very much in the same position as public health work did fifty years ago in its relation to the old purely clinical medicine. In both cases the new ideas had to face the criticism of conservative opponents, and both had, therefore, quickly to justify themselves by demonstrable success. How preventive medicine established its position over half a century ago is familiar to you all. At that time bad housing, the results of the industrial revolution, the prevalence of serious diseases in epidemic form, the amount of illness due to bad water supplies in cities and countries, all offered to the new public health work the opportunity which it was not slow to take advantage of, and upon which it built the national health services which are to-day a fundamental part of the Government activities in every country in the world. International medicine was similarly fortunate in finding at its birth a dramatic opportunity of demonstrating its possibilities to a world at that time still dominated by the national hatreds engendered by the War.

As a result of military operations in the Great War, almost the whole population from Eastern Poland had been driven over the frontiers into Russia. In 1921 the peasants started to return to Poland. Although materially they were almost completely destitute, such clothing as they had was covered with lice. At this time a very severe disease, known as typhus fever, was raging in Russia, where there were half a million cases in 1921 and one and a half million in 1922. Typhus fever is carried by lice, and the return of the Polish peasants in their masses threatened to create a European catastrophe, once the lice in Roumania and Poland became thoroughly infected with typhus fever. It was essential, therefore, to organize a cordon of disinfecting posts right across Europe to kill all the infected lice on the clothing and bodies of the peasants as they arrived. For this cordon to be effective the steps taken by the various countries bordering on Russia had to be co-ordinated, and this co-ordinating, together with the collection of information as to the disease in Russia, was the first piece of work of the League of Nations Epidemic Commission, which was the forerunner of the Health Organization. This work was extremely urgent in character, and not only were huge areas involved, but the numbers of infected peasants arriving daily in Poland made the work one of the first magnitude.

A series of disinfecting posts were created right across Europe on the Russian frontier. All returning refugees were compelled to pass through one or other of these posts, which were situated on the railway lines and main roads. On arrival at the frontier from Russia each refugee train was stopped and the passengers made to strip and leave their clothes in the train, each one being provided with one blanket. Each refugee was then given a bath of paraffin and soft soap in order to kill all the infected lice upon his body. In the meantime the train, with the clothing inside, was backed into a large underground tunnel filled with prussic acid gas, the engine uncoupled and the doors of the tunnel closed. When the bathing was complete, the train was hauled out of the tunnel and the peasants returned to their clothing now sterilized by the prussic acid gas. The immensity of this work may be gathered from the fact that at one of these posts alone we were passing through as many as ten thousand refugees in twenty-four hours.

ii. *The Establishment and Methods of Work of the Health Organization.*

Whilst this demonstration of the practical necessity for international co-operation in medicine was taking place in the countries along the Russian frontier, the Health Organization was being created in Geneva in accordance with Article 23 (f) of the Covenant, by which Members of the League agree 'to take steps in matters of international concern for the prevention and control of disease.'

This was in 1920, and to-day the machinery exists in practically the same form as was created then.

The Health Organization consists of a Health Committee,[1] an Advisory Council (which is the Comité permanent de

[1] In accordance with the Assembly Resolution of last year, the Health Committee is at present undergoing an internal reorganization.

l'Office international d'Hygiène publique), and the Health Section which is the executive organ. The members of the Health Committee are medical experts or senior officials in national public health services.

In order to avoid the scientific discussions of the Committee being hampered by any political considerations, the Members do not represent their Governments and are selected only for their technical qualifications. Consequently, a number belong to countries which are not Members of the League (one being an ex-Surgeon-General of the United States Public Health Service). The whole Committee lays down the programme of work for the Health Section, and gives expert advice on technical questions submitted to it by the League Council. In this work it is assisted by Technical Committees or Conferences of Experts. The Health Section consists of a number of public health specialists, epidemiologists and statisticians of various nationalities, and carries out the programme drawn up by the Committee. It collects information required by the different expert committees, makes preparations for conferences and study tours, and, by correspondence, publications or translations, forms a connecting link between all who are engaged upon research work on the same problems.

Broadly speaking, the different methods by which the Health Organization works can be classified under the following headings :

(a) *The Work of Commissions and Committees of Experts.*

These Commissions are composed of recognized authorities in various countries and work in collaboration with the leading scientific institutes as, for example, the Medical

Research Council in England and the Pasteur Institute in Paris. The Commissions provide means for the general co-ordination of research and for the pooling and comparative study of results in the case of particular diseases. Among the pieces of work carried out by various Commissions may be mentioned the studies on malaria, leprosy, fumigation of ships, rabies, maternal and infantile mortality, cancer, tuberculosis, sleeping sickness, deafness, rural hygiene, housing, nutrition, trachoma, etc.

(b) *The Collection of Information from various Countries with regard particularly to Disease Incidence.*

This is done by the Intelligence Service in Geneva and the Singapore Bureau in the Far East.

(c) *Collaboration with various Governments.*

This comprises the sending to Governments, at their request, of an expert, or a group of experts, to advise or to help the Government concerned in the reconstruction of its Health Service, or in other problems.

(d) *Medical Educational Work, including Collective Study Tours, Individual Study Tours and International Courses in Public Health Subjects.*

(a) *The Work of Commissions and Committees of Experts.*

As it is impossible in a short paper to deal in detail with the work done by the various Commissions and Technical Committees, the object of this address will perhaps best be served by outlining the work of òne or two Commissions as typical of the method of work followed by the Commissions generally.[1]

---

[1] The reports of all the Commissions are constantly appearing as publications of the Health Organization and are obtainable from the Publications Section of the League of Nations at Geneva.

iii. *The Malaria Commission.*

This was one of the first Commissions to be created, and with its subsequent history and future programme may well be taken as an example.

Malaria is one of the most widespread of all illnesses. From the dark tropical forests of South and Central America and Africa to the wide grass plains of Europe and Asia, from the yellow muddy reaches of the Mississippi to the floating reed islands of the delta of the Danube, amongst white, yellow, black and brown peoples indiscriminately, always it is the same disease though with minor differences depending upon the different kind of parasites and upon local and climatic social conditions.   For all these areas the Malaria Commission, representing all the various schools of malariology, is able to pool information and experience acquired by experts all over the world.   To show the extent to which this has already been done, it may be mentioned that in a recent enquiry ninety-three Health Administrations of malaria countries collaborated, representing three-quarters of the population of the whole world, and based on the treatment in the past year of no fewer than one and a half million cases.   The history of this Commission dates from the time immediately after the War when, owing to the absence of men on military duties, the harvests in many parts of Eastern Europe had failed with a resulting weakening of the stamina of the population.   Moreover, the constant movement of troops from malarial to non-malarial districts caused the introduction of malaria amongst already underfed peasant populations.   The result was that the disease became widespread over huge tracts of Europe.   Malaria not only makes the sufferers very ill, but it also establishes a vicious circle. The more malaria there is in a country the less wheat is planted, as the population is too weak to plough and the people become undernourished in consequence. Then more malaria occurs and still less ploughing is done. It was urgently necessary to do something to break this vicious circle, especially in Roumania, Bulgaria, Greece and Yugoslavia, and to introduce into these countries the methods of dealing with malaria which had already proved successful in tropical countries. The Malaria Commission, consisting of well-known experts on malaria who had had experience in India, Africa, Dutch East Indies and elsewhere, was therefore established by the Health Organization to study the best existing practical methods of malaria control, and afterwards to visit the countries in Europe where malaria was widely epidemic, in order to advise the Governments concerned as to the most useful steps to be taken to control it.

Later, in its report on this work, the Malaria Commission emphasized the difficulty presented by the high cost of quinine. One of the principal causes of this is the elaborate process necessary to separate the drug from the cinchona bark in which it grows. The Commission, therefore, proceeded to further work suggested by the necessity for a cheaper efficient substitute. It was quickly found that the extraction of all the alkaloids of cinchona bark without the costly specific separation of quinine produced a very much less expensive drug. The question then arose as to whether the results obtained with this total extract of cinchona bark were as satisfactory as with quinine. Co-ordinating experiments were, therefore, organized in Italy, Roumania, Spain and Yugoslavia to determine the value of certain mixtures of these alkaloids and to compare the results. These experiments, conducted over a period of several years, showed that certain extracts of the bark have a curative value resembling that of quinine. This cheap product could henceforward be used, and will to some extent make up for the insufficient quantity of quinine needed for medical requirements.

Recently it has been found possible to construct chemically a series of substances (atebrin, plasmoquina, etc.) which could be produced very much more cheaply than quinine and appeared at the same time to be of almost equal value in malaria. To study this a further series of comparative experiments in various countries was organized by the Malaria Commission, and experiments were carried out both in hospitals and in the field in Algeria, the Federated Malay States, Italy, Roumania and the u.s.s.r. The report of the Commission on these experiments is at present in the Press.

During its investigation work the Malaria Commission was constantly impressed in each country with the scarcity of doctors who possessed any specialized knowledge in the treatment of malaria. To meet this the Commission organized courses in malariology at Hamburg, London and Paris, followed by practical instruction at the anti-malaria centres in Italy, Spain and Yugoslavia. It was later decided to extend this work by creating a course on the same lines in the Far East, where the conditions are not comparable with those in Europe. As a result three courses have now been held at the College of Medicine in Singapore, with the collaboration of the Government of the Straits Settlements, and these have been followed by practical courses in Indo-China, Java and Malaya. Through scholarships granted by the Health Organization, the

Rockefeller Foundation and Governments, more than three hundred doctors specially engaged in malaria control have been able to attend these courses in Europe and the Far East.

In addition to its work as an Expert Committee, the Commission has also supplied experts to various Governments upon their request. At the request of the Government of Yugoslavia, for example, a member of the Malaria Committee visited that country to investigate the effect of the anti-malaria measures taken. Another expert drew up in Albania a complete plan of campaign against malaria, whilst two of the Commission's experts, at the request of the French Government, visited Corsica and drew up a scheme for reclaiming marsh lands. Experts of the Malaria Commission have also acted as advisers to the Governments of Bulgaria and Greece. Recently, at the request of the Government of British India, the Commission visited the malaria regions of that country. The results were not only of great scientific interest, but are such as can be immediately put into practice in India and tropical countries.

At the present time the Malaria Commission is working particularly on the further investigation of atebrin and plasmoquina and on the possibility of convening an Inter-Governmental Quinine Conference. In another field, fresh studies are also contemplated. These concern the application of methods, known as 'naturalistic,' to modify, by natural means (biological, physiological or chemical), the breeding places of mosquitoes. These methods include the stocking of rivers and stagnant pools with fish, the modification of the physical and chemical character of such water, and the destruction of mosquito larvæ by parasites.

iv. *The Sleeping Sickness Commission.*

Another Commission that was early appointed by the Health Committee had as its mandate the study of sleeping sickness in Central Africa. This is an entirely different illness from the 'sleepy sickness' which occurs in Europe. Sleeping sickness is carried by a special fly—the tsetse fly—and not only affects human beings, but makes it impossible to keep herds of cattle in huge areas of Africa as they, too, die of the disease after being bitten by this fly.

The Sleeping Sickness Commission visited the chief regions in Africa where the disease occurs, with the result that a research laboratory was established with a staff of international workers. But more than this was done. The various Governments of Africa agreed to a form of sleeping sickness 'passport.' As a result, nowadays any native wishing to move from a country in Central Africa, where the disease occurs, to another, or even from one tribal area to another, must be in possession of one of these passports which states whether he has any symptoms of sleeping sickness. Formerly the disease was so dreaded by the natives that the tribes on their own initiative had adopted an effective, if severe, method of preventing this disease from invading new areas. So afraid were they, that any newcomer or native passing through the tribe's country was examined by the witch doctor for the tell-tale swellings in the back of the neck which occur in the early stage of the illness. If any swellings were there—and there are many causes of swellings in the neck, apart from sleeping sickness—the unfortunate man was at once killed. Now, in Africa, to those in possession of a sleeping sickness 'passport,' a visit to the witch doctor is not the same nerve-wracking experience that it must have been formerly.

The Commission also collected scientific information of great value and unanimously recommended certain practical measures for dealing with the disease, such as International Agreements for the supervision of the movements of natives, their treatment, bush clearance as a preventive measure, etc. Later, a Conference of Government representatives was held in Paris to consider the application of the Commission's report. This Conference drew up a programme of investigations to be carried out by the African laboratories and recommended the carrying out of these investigations by the Health Organization.

v. *The Leprosy Commission.*

Leprosy is still widespread over large areas of the world, especially in Asia and South America. Whenever attempts had been made to isolate patients, unless the accommodation offered was attractive, hiding of cases quickly followed. The Leprosy Commission was therefore appointed to consider the question of the diagnosis of the disease and its consequences. The Commission advocated the effective system of voluntary diagnosis and early treatment in out-patients' dispensaries, and at the same time recommended a campaign to spread the knowledge of preventive measures amongst the populations. The Commission also collected information regarding all that was best in the first-class leper settlements of the world, together with the forms of treatment that have proved most satisfactory. This was published and widely circulated to Governments. Today any country in the world wishing to provide humane accommodation for its lepers has, in this report, the full details of how to build and run a leper settlement with the greatest comfort to the patient, the maximum efficiency and the minimum of cost. The need for information of this kind can hardly be over-estimated. It seems almost incredible, but within the last few years I, myself, have seen in Europe, lepers chained in rows to iron rings in a wall like animals, lepers in a barbed-wire entanglement trenched round and guarded by soldiers without any doctors, and lepers landed on a desert, rocky island in the Mediterranean with no amenities of life and no doctor; a ship arriving once a week dumped a week's ration of food, a supply of water and more lepers. Yet these represent the only efforts made by the Governments of three European countries to provide accommodation for their lepers.

vi. *The Cancer Commission.*

This terribly widespread disease occurs not only in human beings of every colour and of every race, but also throughout the animal world. Starting in 1923, the Cancer Commission of the Health Organization has been working along two principal lines. As the result of expert investigations in the various countries of Europe as to the distribution of the disease, much valuable information was gained. It was soon found, for example, in Britain, Italy and the Netherlands, that though cancer occurred almost equally in the women of all three nations, the amount of it and the particular organ of the body affected varied very greatly in the three countries. This led to a long enquiry, which clearly could only be carried out by international collaboration, to determine whether certain

European nationalities were more liable to the disease than others. A difference was actually found between the races —Mediterranean peoples were less liable to cancer—but the difference was not sufficient to explain the variations between the figures of Italy on the one hand and those of England and the Netherlands on the other. So far no satisfactory explanation of this difference has been discovered, but it suggests a line of valuable work towards the ultimate discovery of the cause of the disease. The Cancer Commission has also been engaged for many years on work to determine whether a patient suffering from cancer has a better chance of recovery if treated by operation or by radium and X-rays. Careful records extending over five years are being kept in a large number of cancer hospitals in Great Britain, France, Belgium, Sweden and Italy, of all cases of cancer applying for treatment, whether they are treated by operation or by radium. A note is kept of the extent of the growth at the beginning of treatment, and also how long after first noticing it the patient came to the doctor. Then a description of the operation is given, or if there is no operation, the amount of radium and X-ray treatment given. At the end of five years enquiries are made about each case as to whether the patient has completely recovered, partially recovered, or has died from cancer or some other cause. This work has now been going on for six years, and large numbers of five years' records are now available and are being analysed, so that it will be possible to determine which method offers the best hopes for a patient at different stages of the disease —an operation, treatment with radium or X-rays, or a combination of both.

The above examples will give a general idea of the lines

upon which the various expert committees of the Health Organization work and the methods adopted in connexion with international investigations. The following list of other Commissions and Expert Committees, which have been set up by the Health Organization, is given to illustrate the scope of the work: Reporting Committee for Maternal Welfare; Advisory Commission for the Welfare and Protection of Young People and Children; Reporting Committee for the Hygiene of Children of School Age; Committee for the Study of Medical Education; Reporting Committee for Venereal Diseases; Commission for the Study of Effects of Economic Depression on the Public Life. In addition, technical studies and enquiries are being carried out at the present time on housing, rural hygiene, nutrition, syphilis, hydrophobia, typhus fever, etc.

vii. *The Collection of Information from various Countries with regard particularly to Disease Incidence.*

In the early days of the League Health Organization, when the Epidemic Commission was engaged in its work in preventing typhus fever from entering Europe from Russia, the necessity for the collection of information relating to the diseases existing in each country became of fundamental importance. The Epidemiological Service of the Health Organization was therefore created and began work in 1921, when it published reports on the health situation in Eastern Europe, with special reference to typhus fever in Russia and Poland. Later, these reports were extended so as to include information relating first to Europe and then gradually to the whole world. This work has grown steadily and rapidly, and today the Epidemiological Service of the League, working in close collaboration with the Comité permanent de l'Office international d'Hygiène publique in Paris, collects epidemiological information covering no less than 72 per cent of the population of the whole world. This information is published weekly and is sent to all health administrations all over the world.

Originally the sole object of the Epidemiological Service was to supply information to the authorities of each country on the health situation in neighbouring countries, particularly with regard to the occurrence of typhus fever, small-pox, cholera, plague, malaria, diphtheria, etc. Soon, however, the importance of these data from the point of view of epidemiological research became evident, and it was realized that if they were co-ordinated it would make possible much investigation into the geographical and seasonal incidence of disease and its relation to climatic conditions. Very valuable work has since been done by the Epidemiological Service along these lines.

It was, however, particularly in the Far East that the need for rapid information as to the existence and spread of epidemics was so essential. At the end of the last century plague from Hongkong was carried by ships to important ports of all the neighbouring countries, and in British India alone this disease has since caused more than ten million deaths, whilst in the last ten years over a million cases of cholera have occurred in addition. It is not surprising, therefore, that in 1925, at a Conference of Far Eastern Administrations held at Singapore, it was decided to establish a bureau of the Health Organization at Singapore under an Advisory Council including representatives of the heads of the public health services of the various countries of the East. The Governments in East Africa, India, the Malay States, the Dutch East Indies, China, Japan, Australia, French Indo-China, the Philippines, the islands of the South Pacific, Siam, etc., now transmit regularly to the Singapore office, daily or weekly, according to the urgency, a statement of the number of cases of serious infectious diseases occurring in each port in their country during the preceding week. Based on this report a weekly broadcast is made by wireless through the French Government station at Saigon, Indo-China, and is relayed by Government wireless stations in Malabar (Java), Hong-kong, Shanghai, Tokyo, Karachi, Bombay and Tananarive in Madagascar for East Africa. The message gives the ports infected with plague, malaria or smallpox in the preceding week and also notification received from steamers of cases of infectious diseases occurring on board at sea. This wireless message is sent out on short and long waves all over the East from the Suez Canal to the Panama Canal and from Vladivostock to Melbourne. It is picked up by ships and enables them to know whether the ports to which they are proceeding are infected with plague or cholera, and, similarly, enables health authorities in the various ports throughout the East to know which arriving ships have come from infected ports, and so enables them to take the necessary precautions against the spread of disease. This work is considered of such value to the various Governments that the Singapore office of the Health Organization receives subsidies from the Governments in the Far East, apart from their annual contribution to the League itself, and also from countries non-Members of the League.

The information as to the existence of epidemics is also sent by wireless from Singapore to Geneva, where similar information regarding infectious diseases in all parts of the world is received and published weekly.

viii. *Collaboration with various Governments.*

The Government of any country can, at its own request, benefit by the information available at Geneva and by the experience of the experts of the Technical Committees of the Health Organization, or it may, at any time, request the Health Organization to place experts at its disposal to carry out specific tasks—an opportunity which has been frequently used. Governments have requested opinions as to the best measures of coping with malaria (Albania), syphilis (Bulgaria), an epidemic of dengue (Greece), and also advice regarding hospital reorganization (Irish Free State) and nutritional problems (Chile).

Frequently the request is for advice on the reorganization of the public health administration of a whole country.

Assistance on these lines has already been given to Bulgaria, China, Czechoslovakia, Greece and Liberia. Experts sent by the Health Organization first make a detailed survey of the problem and of the social and economic conditions of the population, and upon this is drawn up a report with recommendations which, after approval by the Health Committee, is forwarded to the Governments concerned.

The work entailed by some of these requests is very varied. For example, in the mountainous country of Bolivia we carried out a survey which lasted six months, using for travelling an aeroplane lent by the Government, which involved regular flying at 23,000 feet among the high peaks of the Andes, journeys on horseback for weeks on the upper reaches of the Amazon and the crossing of the Andes three times on muleback. In Liberia much of our work was in the bush on foot with only head porterage. In Czechoslovakia, by way of a complete change from Liberia, we carried out some of the surveys of the mountainous regions on skis, and in Greece on horseback.

In each case the problem was investigated in detail, the recommendations made and transmitted to the Government concerned.

ix. *Medical Educational Work, including Collective Study Tours, Individual Study Tours and International Courses in Public Health Subjects.*

With a view to supplying public health workers with information regarding work in other countries, the Health Organization published a series of monographs on organization and working of the public health services in different countries. These brochures contained data on the administrative regulations, health legislation and principal health problems of those countries, and supplied information on the co-operation of private associations with the public health authorities. Furthermore, in order to keep the various authorities up to date, the Health Section published the International Health Year-Book, which contains an annual summary of the progress made in different countries and of any important new health measures introduced.

In addition the Health Organization arranges both collective and individual study tours for doctors holding official positions, in order to enable them to study specific problems. These tours cover a large number of various branches of medicine, some being for public health officials, others for specialists in tuberculosis, infant hygiene, school hygiene, health administration of ports, statistics, etc. More than 700 officials belonging to States Members of the League and also to a certain number of non-Member States, such as the United States of America, have participated in these interchanges of health personnel. Nearly all the countries in Europe as well as Latin America, the United States of America, Canada, West Africa, India and Japan, have been visited and have sent their officials to the study tours.

x. *Conclusion.*

In a relatively short space, considering the present and potential magnitude of the work, I have attempted to outline the principal activities of the Health Organization. I have tried to show the extent to which the work has developed, the fundamental and logical necessity for its existence, and to hint at the great future before it.

The rapidity of modern transport and the great amount of travelling done by all classes have both served to increase the need for international collaboration, if the fullest advantage is to be taken of our own and our neighbour's knowledge in the control of disease. There can be no question of the value of international co-operation in the control of epidemics, in the co-ordination of research in all countries, and of the pooling of information from different countries which have had to face similar problems.

It was in recognition of this fact that the Health Organization of the League was created and is maintained by the Governments Members of the League of Nations.

In addition, the Health Organization maintains the closest scientific collaboration with, as well as receives considerable financial contributions from, Governments which are not Members of the League. No higher tribute than this could be paid to the necessity for the Health Organization's work, no fuller appreciation given of the international work already accomplished in medicine or greater official guarantee afforded of confidence in its future achievements.

CHAPTER VI

A WORLD ECONOMIC SURVEY

by

J. B. CONDLIFFE

Member of the Economic Intelligence Service of the
League of Nations Secretariat

WE have witnessed the disappearance of many political and economic landmarks during the past few years. The world is a very different place from what it was ten years ago, though in many respects not perhaps so different from what it was a hundred years ago. Much of the stress and strain of our time is obviously due to readjustment of the broken post-War system of international relations. The immediate post-War settlement has clearly broken down. Not only have its political arrangements changed, but the attempt to reconstruct a post-War economic world on the pre-War model has also failed. We are in the midst of a period of rapid reorganization, during which it is difficult to distinguish what is temporary from what is permanent change. It is, nevertheless, worth inquiring how much of what we have thought was essential in international organization has been carried away with the post-War superstructure.

This paper is not concerned with the political aspects of the present situation, which are admirably treated elsewhere in this volume. The aim here is to present a brief survey of the economic situation. Such a survey would have been much more difficult, if not impossible, for the hardiest lecturer before the existence of the Economic Intelligence Service of the League, which is itself a fact worth thinking about. Thanks to the regular painstaking collection of statistical data concerning various aspects of economic life in all the countries which provide such data, it is now possible for a group of international economists to assemble, standardize and analyse economic movements quantitatively for the world as a whole and for its constituent parts. The economists who do so are international not only in being drawn from different nationalities, but also in being able, nay, in being compelled, to interpret their data from a non-national view-point. Necessarily, as the data from one country fit into those from another, they see the world as a developing economic organism. While there remain many gaps in our information, it is now possible to say that whatever material of value exists in any country is collected and placed in its proper international setting. The mere standardization of this data, calculating index-numbers on a common base period, and converting weights, measures and currencies to common units, is an important contribution to statistical analysis, as any economist will testify who has tried to do research into international economic problems with his own resources. It is not lack of information from which the world is suffering at the moment. Nor is it lack of understanding of the information collected. There seems no need to add further machinery for fact-finding and analysis. What is needed in the economic field is action, and action depends upon prior political agreement.

i. *Unheeded Warnings.*

What is the picture of recent economic development which is presented by the information collected by the Economic Intelligence Service? In order to answer this question briefly and, I trust, intelligibly, I propose to ask and tentatively answer three other questions which have a direct bearing upon the main topic of discussion at this Institute. For some time past we have become habituated to economists and committees of experts, warning us that if certain trends of economic development continued or became aggravated, the world would be poorer and even worse disasters might ensue. I select only one of these warnings since it was issued by the imposing Preparatory Commission of Experts that drew up the 'Draft Annotated Agenda' for the Monetary and Economic Conference of 1933. After outlining the damage done by the depression to international economic relations, they drew attention to the beginnings of recovery that were evident in the closing months of 1932, and ended their brief introductory survey with these words:

'Nevertheless, recovery will be halting and restricted if unaccompanied by broad measures of reconstruction. Three years of world-wide dislocation have generated a vast network of restraints upon the normal conduct of business. In the field of international trade, prohibitions, quotas, clearing agreements, exchange restrictions—to mention only some of the most widely employed forms of regulation—throttle business enterprise and individual initiative. Defensively intended, and in many instances forced by unavoidable monetary and financial emergencies, these measures have developed into a state of virtual economic warfare. It is not only in the field of trade that this tension exists. In the difficult sphere of international monetary and currency relations and in the world capital markets, free international co-operation has given place to complex and harassing regulations designed to safeguard national interests. If a full and durable recovery is to be affected, this prevailing conflict of national economies must be resolved.

'The measures to be adopted to this end constitute the problem which the Governments must shortly face in London. In essence, the necessary programme is one of economic disarmament. In the movement towards economic reconciliation the armistice was signed at Lausanne ; the London Conference must draft the Treaty of Peace. Failure in this critical undertaking threatens a world-wide adoption of ideals of national self-sufficiency which cut unmistakably athwart the lines of economic development. Such a choice would shake the whole system of international finance to its foundations, standards of living would be lowered, and the social system as we know it could hardly survive. These developments, if they occur, will be the result, not of any inevitable natural law, but of the failure of human will and intelligence to devise the necessary guarantees of political and economic international order. The responsibility of Governments is clear and inescapable.'

This is rather strong language. Of course something must be allowed for the desire, one might even say the anxiety, of the experts to get their Governments and their peoples into the proper frame of mind to make the Conference work. The Conference in fact was a failure; but disaster has not yet ensued. This is rather typical of the situation in recent years. It seems clear that, in practically every country, Governments have done what, in the eyes of the experts, they ought not to have done, and have left undone those things which they ought to have done. There have been very marked departures from what used formerly to be regarded as essential principles of international economic organization. After some years of exchange instability it is not yet possible to reconstruct an international monetary standard, and the necessity for doing so has been widely questioned. There is today little long-term international investment, but a great amount of short-term vagabond capital that moves nervously from one financial centre to another. International trade, though increasing again, is much less than it was and is still subject to complicated and effective restrictions. In various national economies even more startling developments have occurred. Budgets have been deliberately unbalanced, monetary policy has followed distinctly unorthodox lines and there has been an increasing range and effectiveness of Government intervention in economic activity. The precedence of political over economic objectives is very clear in some cases.

Yet, however clouded the political horizon may be, there is at the present time, and has been for some years, accumulating evidence of economic prosperity. My three questions, therefore, in the order of importance and difficulty are : Were the experts wrong in their diagnosis? Or has there been some exaggeration of the departure from and some return to sound economic principles? Or, finally, is the present appearance of prosperity deceptive?

I fear that my tentative answers to these questions must be somewhat in the nature of Solomon's judgment, or perhaps the Dodo's when after deep sub-conscious meditation he concluded that 'all had won and all must have prizes.' In other words, there is some pertinence in all these questions.

ii. *Was the Diagnosis False?*

I have already suggested that in phrasing the dilemma with which they confronted the Governments, the experts who prepared the Draft Annotated Agenda for the Monetary and Economic Conference were probably moved by a desire to prepare the ground for the action they deemed necessary at the time. In the event, however, the failure of the Conference to act did not produce a wholesale reversion to policies of national isolation and self-sufficiency. There was, it is true, a definite trend in that direction in many countries, and notably in Germany; but on the other hand some of the most powerful Governments acted with great moderation and constantly bore international considerations in mind when framing their national policies. The dollar was provisionally stabilized in terms of gold at the end of January 1934, and has not varied since. After March 1935, also, sterling was maintained virtually stable with the dollar. Since many other currencies were, if not pegged, at least maintained at stable parities with the dollar and sterling, there has been in fact a wide area of exchange stability for almost three years now. The devaluations and depreciations that accompanied the Tripartite Agreement of September 1936 are best described as an alignment of other currencies with this stable group. Despite the subsequent difficulties which prevented France from reaping the full benefit from devaluation, the events of September 1936 brought a substantial redressment of international price equilibria. The following table, showing the relative levels of wholesale prices corrected for exchange depreciation in June 1937 as compared with June 1936, shows that there has been a notable levelling down of price-levels that were previously high and a levelling up of those price-levels that were previously low. Too much importance should not be attached to the relatively high levels shown for the countries practising exchange control, since in fact much of the foreign commerce of those countries is conducted at exchange rates below the official parities. The spread of the wholesale-price index numbers (expressed in terms of a common gold unit) was much less in June 1937 than it had been a year earlier, and a greater number of the national indices were grouped closely around the mean. There were still fairly wide discrepancies in the purchasing power parities between certain countries, but it must be remembered that they are all calculated with reference to the relationships existing in 1929 which were not necessarily in equilibrium. The recent movements, upward in the raw-material producing countries and downward in the countries which have lately devalued, have been in the direction of a more stable equilibrium, and this has been made possible by the stability of the exchange rates over a wide area.

Gold wholesale-price levels, June 1937, compared with June 1936:

(1929 = 100)

Hungary	.	78 (70)	Danzig .	.	62 (58)
Germany	.	77 (76)	Portugal	.	60 (53)
Austria .	.	70 (67)	Czechoslovakia	.	59 (64)
Albania.	.	63 (62)	France .	.	59 (60)
Bulgaria	.	63 (56)	Belgium	.	59 (48)
Poland .	.	63 (56)	United Kingdom		58 (50)
Netherlands.	.	62 (62)	Norway	.	58 (50)
Turkey .	.	62 (61)	Latvia .	.	56 (71)

Switzerland	56 (65)	China	51 (43)
Sweden	56 (48)	Estonia	51 (47)
Italy	55 (66)	South Africa	50 (50)
Yugoslavia	55 (50)	New Zealand	49 (46)
U.S.A.	54 (49)	Egypt	45 (44)
Finland	54 (48)	Chile	45 (36)
Denmark	54 (47)	Australia	44 (41)
Roumania	54 (55)	British India	44 (39)
Canada	52 (45)	Peru	43 (55)
Greece	52 (47)	Japan	37 (31)

The economic experts seem also to have under-estimated the ingenuity of private enterprise in adapting itself to new forms of Government regulation and control. The instinct of self-preservation, which is the foundation upon which the capitalist system is built, is exceedingly persistent and tenacious. Given even a modicum of stability in the regulations to which it must conform, it accommodates itself quickly and with surprising readiness to new situations. While the restrictive effect of regulations cannot by any means be ignored, their rapid changes are even more destructive of enterprise. As Alice remarked to the Caterpillar, the business world does not so much mind the hindrances placed in its way as it objects to " changing so often." On the other hand, there has been perhaps some tendency to think in terms of familiar institutions and practices, to distrust new forms of social control and regulation, and to under-estimate the force of other than economic motives. As Governments, bowing to popular pressure, have extended their intervention into fields formerly left to private enterprise, the well-known incentives to economic effort may have been weakened in certain directions, but the social fabric has not crumbled. There has been perhaps a tendency to think too much of finance rather than production and equitable distribution, and of trade rather than employment. Implicit in this tendency is the assumption that property rights and customary practices were necessary for efficiency. Time will show how far the restriction of these rights and practices have in fact impaired the functioning of the economic system ; but there is little doubt of the popular will to put such social objectives as economic security, and more equitable distribution of wealth, before maximum production. One may, however, go farther and point to a social development of immense significance in the evident capacity and even relish of great masses of people for the absorption of propaganda. National propaganda in particular has persuaded whole nations to accept regimentation and submit to sacrifices that have hitherto been almost impossible to conceive except under the emotional stress of war conditions.

iii. *How far has there been a Departure from Sound Principles?*

More important, however, than the correctness of the experts' diagnoses and prognoses is the second question : How far in fact has there been a departure from sound economic principles in recent years? Part of the answer to that question depends upon the objectives towards which economic activity is directed. If national security or prestige is regarded as of more importance than comfort, it may be sound procedure to accept limitations which reduce economic efficiency. In the same way, a people may be prepared to risk some loss of wealth in order to secure a greater degree of social justice, though in fact it is probable that a greater measure of economic equality will in the long run increase rather than diminish production.

There seem to be two main areas in which there have recently been extensive innovations in respect of Government regulation. The first is in the labour market broadly defined, and the second is in international economic relations. Intervention is not new in either field, but its scope has been so greatly extended in recent years as to warrant its being regarded almost as a new phenomenon. There has been an increasing tendency to attach importance to such conceptions as minimum labour standards, both of wages and of working conditions, the provision of employment, the relief of unemployment, and in general the assurance of a reasonable standard of life as a social right. So far has this tendency developed that the right to a decent minimum standard of life is coming to have the same importance in economic organization as the longer established rights of property. Necessarily intervention in this field has led to an extension of Government control over prices, and the chief means employed by Governments to afford employment and relief have directly affected the capital market and the rate of interest.

In passing, it may be noticed that, new as the devices may be, the problems are old. Indeed the extension of Government intervention is in many respects a re-assertion of economic and social ideas, such as that of the just price, which were characteristic of the early modern age. Nearly fifty years ago an acute observer remarked of New Zealand's pioneer ventures in State Socialism that they represented a reversal of the historic process described by Maine as characteristic of the nineteenth century, and were leading back again from contract to status. The recent limitation of private enterprise is tending in the same direction, and is undoubtedly backed by majority opinion in most countries.

The most doubtful aspects of State intervention, however, arise from the fact that in practical politics the pressure of group interests rather than principles of social justice are apt to determine the policies pursued. The result is to create a new series of privileged positions with a consequent distortion of economic organization, not always in the general interest. The most destructive development in this direction has been the assertion of the all-powerful State interest as an end in itself. Armament policies are the clearest instances of this subordination of the average individual to the supposed needs of the State. Wherever the general is sacrificed to particular interests there is economic distortion and loss; but the greatest damage to economic life in this direction is coming from this misdirection of effort and resources to armaments and to the achievement of great national self-sufficiency. For a time the secondary effects of Government expenditure stimulate production and employment; but in the long run it cannot add to the wealth of nations to divert resources from construction to destruction or to produce expensively what might be imported more cheaply.

It is evident, therefore, that the answer to my second question must be mixed. There is no reason to believe that in the long run measures to give social security and a greater measure of socal justice, if prudently introduced and efficiently administered, need hinder economic productivity. On the contrary, long experience, for example with factory legislation, leads to the belief that a community gains in efficiency from paying attention to the human needs of labour. It is the abuses of Government intervention, in the interest of sectional groups, and above all in the aggrandisement of the State, that distort economic organization and detract from its efficiency. Already the costs of such abuses are quite evident. Costs of living rising faster than wages and still more than salaries and fixed incomes, delays in the satisfaction of individual requirements, higher prices for motor-cars because there is a shortage of steel, rising food prices because food imports are restricted, are symptoms of this trend. Every generation pays for its own mistakes in this way by concealed but none the less real reductions if not of the actual standard of living, at least of the standard that might be attained. In addition, particularly when monetary policy is used to facilitate State expenditures, there is added the risk of industrial disorganization leading to an aggravation of business fluctuations, and a burden of new debt which makes future generations pay again.

There is much the same story to tell of Government intervention in the second field, where it has recently been widely extended—the field of international economic relations. In the crises of the post-War period the international monetary and trading relations which proved so profitable in the pre-War period have been seriously impaired. The stability of the foreign exchanges, which formerly provided a workable equivalent of an international currency, was destroyed by successive currency depreciations and has proved difficult to restore. New and very effective trade barriers were erected and international specialization was thereby handicapped. The long-term foreign investment which developed new countries and enriched the lenders was almost completely paralysed. The costs of this impairment of international specialization, though masked by national recoveries largely based upon the debasement of currencies, have been very real. It is obviously uneconomic to grow subsidized wheat unprofitably at high cost when subsidies are being paid elsewhere to restrict wheat-growing in areas where conditions are favourable and costs are low. It is equally costly to produce manufactured goods on a small scale when they could be produced much more effectively and cheaply by mass production methods. Where economic isolation has been carried furthest, consumers are eating bread the constituents of which are adulterated, wearing clothes the quality of which is lowered by an admixture of substitute materials, and going without the variety of commodities, and particularly the new manufactures towards which demand turns as standards of living rise. Price differences between national economies were increased alarmingly during the period of greatest trade restriction.

It is in this field, however, that there have recently been the most encouraging signs of a return to more sensible economic organization. Mention has already been made of the greater degree of exchange stability that has for the last two or three years been established over a wide and important trading area. The fear of further currency depreciation has been much reduced. This in itself has made possible a tentative approach to the liberalizing and relaxation of the extraordinary trade restrictions that were built up during the depression. Formal action has not been unimportant. Particular attention should be drawn to three initiatives in this direction. After the Tripartite Monetary Agreement of September 1936, immediate action was taken in many of the devaluing countries to reduce or abolish certain quotas and exceptional duties and in some cases to lower tariffs. While these mitigations of trade restrictions did not go as far as was at one time hoped and did not evoke any great response in other countries, they were a step in the right direction. As shortages of certain raw materials developed in the first half of 1937 also, there were many instances of the reduction or abolition of import duties, for example in iron and steel. The Oslo Agreement, by which a group of northern European countries agreed upon the abolition of certain quotas and the reduction of certain duties to facilitate mutual trade, was a further initiative designed not only to increase trade among the Powers concerned, but to open the door to an extension of the concessions. Belgium and the Netherlands extended their concessions under this agreement by giving the benefit of the most-favoured-nation clause to France, the United Kingdom and Germany. While no other countries have yet adhered to the agreement it remains a means of extending trade.

The most important development, however, has been the negotiation of reciprocal trade treaties by the United States—perhaps the most far-reaching and courageous piece of economic statesmanship in recent years. By these agreements both imports to and exports from the United States have been considerably increased, and a substantial breach has been made not only in the high tariff of that country but also in other tariffs. It is particularly significant that these treaties have encouraged the trend in the United States towards a passive import balance of commodity trade as befits a great creditor nation. In years to come this trade treaty programme may well be regarded as a landmark in the economic evolution, not only of the United States but of a new international trading system in which that country will play a larger rôle. The benefits of increased American imports facilitated by the application of most-favoured-nation treatment have extended to a great many countries, including most of the agricultural countries of Central and Southern Europe, whose international accounts have been greatly improved by freer access to free-exchange markets and by rising price-levels. If, as is to be hoped, the negotiations now in progress for a treaty or series of treaties with the United Kingdom and the British Dominions are brought to a successful conclusion, the gain to world trade will be considerable.

Besides such formal action there has also been a substantial freeing of trade by administrative action. In a great number of countries exchange control has been relaxed, quota systems have been liberalized and exchange clearings modified so as to permit a freer play of private trading enterprise. The administrative factor in trade restrictions has been so great that this tendency to looser control is very important. In some cases the way has been prepared for the ultimate removal of exchange control in the manner pioneered by Austria. Turkey has abolished its quota system, and there is a general tendency not only for clearing agreements to be replaced by the more liberal payments agreements, but for the agricultural countries both of Europe and of South America to enlarge their trade with the free-exchange countries.

The beneficial results of more stable exchanges, freer trading facilities and rising prices are already apparent, not only in the improved monetary situation of the agricultural debtor countries, but in the returning prospects of debt settlement. In some of the South American countries there has been a tendency for the uncontrolled exchange rates to appreciate while imports are increasing and balances are accumulating abroad. Brazil has even bought gold. The British Dominions and India, as well as other countries in the sterling area, have built up their sterling assets very considerably and some of them have repaid substantial amounts of external debt. The debtor countries of Europe have been placed in a position to improve their payments on account of debt, and Hungary has been able to make an acceptable offer compounding its League loan obligations and 'stand-still' short-term debts. There has even been some revival of long-term international lending. For the most part this has taken the form of direct industrial investment as, for example, by the building or extension of branch factories, assembly plants or new factories. The replacement of coffee by cotton-growing and the erection of cotton factories in Brazil is a case in point, as indeed is the rapid industrial development in South America generally. There has also been some extension of medium-term credit as witnessed by China's recent successes in floating loans in various European centres. Both Switzerland and the Netherlands have begun again to float long-term loans for foreign countries.

iv. *Is the Present Appearance of Prosperity Deceptive?*

Finally, some attention must be paid to the last of my three questions—Is the present appearance of prosperity real and likely to prove of a lasting character? No economist at the present time is likely to venture a definite opinion concerning the duration of the trade and rearmament boom. In some countries where recovery has been in progress for a long time there are symptoms of disequilibria—rising costs of production, including interest rates, freight rates, raw material prices and wages—that in the past have heralded a cyclical recession. But there are new factors to be considered—an increased degree of Government intervention, more flexible monetary policies, the upward movement of recovery in important areas where the turning-point came late, and reviving international trade. There is no possibility of accurate prediction when undetermined political factors play such a rôle as they now do.

One may, however, draw attention to certain important qualifications of the present apparent prosperity. In the first place statistical measurements disclose much greater production than in recent years; but it must be remembered that a great deal of leeway was lost during the depression. World industrial production in 1936 was about 6 per cent greater than it had been in 1925-29. If the normal pre-War rate of progress, generally reckoned as 3 per cent per annum had been steadily maintained, however, in the years 1929-36, the percentage would have been 28. If production had continued to increase at the rate of 4.4 per cent per annum as it did in the years 1925-29, the percentage would have been 48. If the calculation is carried back to 1913, the ground lost in the War period and the post-War crises is seen to be much greater. Nor does the facile criticism that greater production is not a final test of economic welfare carry very much conviction. Obviously there is need for more equitable distribution of wealth and for greater leisure; but in a world where so much poverty exists and where standards of living are so much lower than we have a right to expect, the check to production has meant a real loss of welfare.

Then too, the cost, particularly of the dislocation of international trade, has been concentrated heavily upon certain areas and a relatively small number of workers. Sir William Beveridge has written of two Britains, the Britain of the south which is enjoying the new prosperity, and the Britain of the north and west which still suffers from the impoverishment of the export industries. Long-term unemployment in Great Britain—unemployment that has lasted for twelve months or more—was $6\frac{1}{2}$ times as great in September 1936 than it had been seven years earlier, and was borne by a group of workers estimated to number 350,000. It is true that unemployment relief has kept them from stark poverty, but monetary payments are no solution of their problems.

Finally, it must be emphasized that, underlying the whole recovery movement, there has been a cheapening of currencies the effects of which are probably only in their early stages. In years to come the period through which we are passing will probably rank with the 'great debasements' of history. I am sometimes asked where the resources come from that have enabled Governments to proceed with vast new expenditures for armaments and other purposes. The answer, broadly, is that the creditors pay part of the real cost and the rest is provided by the new production created by the utilization of hitherto unemployed labour and materials. Among the creditors one must include all who stand to lose by rising prices—wage-earners whose costs of living rise, fixed-income receivers, the holders of superannuation, pension or insurance rights. A considerable redistribution of income is inevitable in a period of rising prices, and it seems probable that we are only at the inception of such a process. It was not only inevitable but probably in the long run beneficial that the great debasement should have occurred. This is the way in which intolerable burdens of past indebtedness are usually thrown off; but we should be clear as to who pays the price. Moreover, as prices rise enterprise benefits as creditor rights diminish; but opportunities for speculation increase, and this brings the risk of aggravating the fluctuations to which our industrial system seems subject. The great problems of policy confronting our generation centre round two related aspects of these monetary developments. They are the reconstruction of an orderly system of international economic co-operation so as to provide a wider basis for spreading the risks of industrial fluctuation while at the same time drawing the maximum benefits from international specialization, and the evolution of monetary policies adequate to the task of liquidating past obligations by reducing their real value as prices rise without allowing the price rise to get out of hand and degenerate into a speculative boom.

CHAPTER VII

SOCIAL AND ECONOMIC CHANGES UNDER THE NEW DEAL

by
CARTER GOODRICH
United States Labour Commissioner, Geneva

i. *Introduction.*

I AM very glad to have the privilege of contributing to this book. I must, however, begin with two disclaimers. In the first place, I should make it clear that I am not writing in any official capacity. My views represent no one but myself, and I hope that you will think of my remarks rather as the speculations of an economic historian on leave than as the statements of a Government official. In the second place, I shall have to confess that I am in no position to bring you the latest word on the quite contemporary problem which I have been assigned. I suggested to your director that a man who had spent the past year in Geneva was hardly qualified to report on the current events of a scene that changes as rapidly as that of the United States under the New Deal. But he seemed willing to take the risk, and I shall do my best to turn this limitation into an advantage. Since I cannot pretend to write as a first-hand observer of the last negotiations in the corridors of Congress or the last clash on the picket lines of the steel towns, I shall emphasize instead only the very broadest outlines of the changes that have taken place during the Roosevelt Administration. Perhaps in this way they may stand out more clearly in their historical and international setting.

Certainly the contrast is sufficiently striking if we compare the social policies of the American Government today and the present labour situation in the United States with those which prevailed during the decade of the 1920's. The first illustration is suggested by the arrival in Geneva this week [1] of one of the most distinguished men in American public life to resume his position as an Assistant Director at the International Labour Office. In the earlier period the United States was not a member of the International Labour Organization, and the argument was frequently made in its debates that such-and-such an industry could not well be regulated, or such-and-such a measure could not safely be adopted, because employment in the United States could not be brought within the scope of the regulations. Now, as you all know, the United States is a full-fledged member, whose increasing activity is typified by Governor Winant's coming, and it is no secret that its influence within the organization is being exerted on the side of increasing boldness in the adoption of international labour legislation.

ii. *The Trade Union Movement in America.*

No less striking are the changes at home, of which the new front at Geneva is symptomatic. If one surveyed American trade unionism in the United States during the 'twenties, it was obvious that the percentage of workers organized was considerably less than that in the older industrial countries of Western Europe, or in such new

[1] August 15 to 21, 1937.

countries as Australia and New Zealand. Moreover, the trade unions were failing to grow in a period of prosperity —a phenomenon which was new and surprising even for the United States. At the same time there was a marked growth on the part of a rival form of organization, the employee representation plan or so-called 'company union,' initiated from the management side and in each case confined to the employees of a single firm. This, indeed, was only one of a number of ingenious devices of labour management—sometimes involving genuine and substantial improvements in the conditions of work—that were being proliferated during this period by the experts in personnel administration. A number of observers believed that the development of this sort of 'welfare capitalism' would avert and make unnecessary the growth of a really formidable labour movement. Two facts, in any case, were clearly evident. Throughout American industry the initiative in the field of industrial relations rested at least as often with management as with labour. And in the industries thought of as most characteristically 'modern' or 'American'—such as steel and automobiles—the employers were free to pursue their policies almost entirely unhampered by union organization.

The present picture is very different. Now, as you know, there come from the United States two kinds of news of the union movement. One is concerned with its bitter internal controversy. The older leadership of the American Federation of Labour, whose President is William Green, is being threatened by a powerful group of unions banded together under the chairmanship of John L. Lewis in the Committee for Industrial Organization. The latter have not yet been formally expelled from the A.F. of L. and the C.I.O. has not yet declared itself a rival and parallel federation; but these actions may be taken at any moment, and the conflict could hardly rage more vigorously if it had already reached this point.

The issues are not altogether easy to state. No doubt the conflict is partly a matter of the ambitions of rival chieftains. Sometimes it is described as one between the conservatism of the A.F. of L. and the radicalism of the C.I.O. In so far as this description is accurate, it is mainly because the C.I.O. is somewhat more of what would in Great Britain be called a 'ginger group'; the general philosophy prevailing in both factions would still seem conservative to most European labour leaders. More often it is described as a conflict between the 'craft' unionism of the American Federation of Labour and the 'industrial' unionism of the Committee for Industrial Organization. This statement also needs qualification. On the one hand, the Secretary of the C.I.O. is a member of the distinctly non-industrial Typographical Union; and on the other hand, the A.F. of L. has long since included a number of industrial unions as well as a larger number organized on the basis of trade or craft. Oddly enough, both Lewis and Green are members of the same industrial union of coal-miners. Nevertheless, the statement contains an important element of truth. The principal charge brought by the C.I.O. against the older leadership was that it had failed to press vigorously enough for the organization of the workers in the modern mass-production industries, where 'crafts' in the old sense scarcely exist; and the principal plank in the Lewis platform is the organization of these workers on an industrial basis.

As to the outcome of the conflict, I shall venture no prediction. It certainly will not be settled in any near

future by the collapse or complete defeat of either of the
parties. The A.F. of L., which still in all probability
controls the larger number of wage-earners, has strong-
holds in the building trades, and in parts of the metal and
printing trades, which the newer movement cannot seriously
threaten. On the other hand, the C.I.O.—whatever may
happen to its many recent converts—can hardly be shaken
in its hold on the powerful and ably-led unions of clothing
workers, or on the United Mine Workers, which is the
largest union on the continent. But it is still much too
early, and Geneva is much too far away, to judge whether
the controversy will be ended by compromise, or whether
the American labour movement for some time to come will
consist of two rival bodies of roughly comparable strength.

But this whole story, as I have said, is only one of the two
sorts of American union news. For all its dramatic quality,
and for all its real seriousness, it must not be allowed to
obscure the second point, which after all is of somewhat
more central importance in the present discussion. That
is the fact of the great advance in the membership and
power of American trade unions during the Roosevelt
Administration.

The increases in membership began in the earliest days of
the New Deal, and have continued since the internal controversy developed. They have accrued to the unions still
supporting Green as well as to those that have followed
Lewis. Within twelve months after the signing of the
National Industrial Recovery Act, well over 600,000 new
members joined the unions, and the second year registered
a growth of nearly 300,000.[1] Since then the rate of increase

[1] Leo Wolman, *Ebb and Flow in Trade Unionism*, National Bureau
of Economic Research, Inc., N.Y., 1936, pp. 147-48.

has again gone up, and the two greatest single triumphs of labour were won early in the present year, both by the Committee for Industrial Organization. In the automobile industry, after a series of spectacular 'sit-down' strikes, and in the steel industry perhaps more surprisingly without the necessity of a strike, the C.I.O. succeeded in securing contracts with the largest and most powerful companies. Even this, to be sure, does not mean that the battle for trade union recognition in the United States has been fully won. Though the recent campaigns have forced into collective bargaining many an angry and surprised employer who had vowed never to let an outsider interfere with the running of his business, there are still a considerable number who stand out. Henry Ford is as yet unbeaten in automobiles, and some of the smaller companies in steel now have the upper hand in a sanguinary encounter with the organizing committee. But to any realistic labour leader, who knew American industry in the 'twenties, the bringing of General Motors and U.S. Steel under union contract would have seemed a revolutionary and almost unbelievable achievement.

iii. *Government and Industry in the U.S.A.*

Such rapid changes in the labour field could not have taken place except for a similar and related contrast in the policies of the American Government. During the 'twenties we elected a national administration on the slogan 'Less Government in Business,' and this of course was in a nation which was already more individualistic in public policy than any other industrial country, and in which even the most obviously enforced departures from *laisser-*

faire had all to be explained and defended in individualistic terms. Consider the situation in the field of labour legislation. The courts had decided that the Federal Government could not regulate the employment of children. No one thought seriously that the Federal Government had the power to regulate hours and wages in general industry, or to set up a comprehensive system of old age pensions. Even a State could not constitutionally enforce a minimum wage. Neither the nation nor any State had attempted to establish insurance for the unemployed. Finally, the legal position of the trade unions, though too diverse and too complex to summarize briefly, was, it is safe to say, less favourable than in any other great democracy.

The elements of contrast are almost too familiar to require citation. It is scarcely necessary to do more than refer to the attempt to regulate trade practices as well as labour conditions through the National Recovery Administration; to the far-reaching control of agriculture exercised through the Agricultural Adjustment Administration and the Resettlement Administration; to the work of federal relief which involved for the first time the assumption of national responsibility for the victims of unemployment and which included the largest and most diversified programme of work relief which has ever been attempted; to the Tennessee Valley Authority, as the boldest of a number of attempts to combine public works with regional reconstruction; and to the Securities Exchange Commission, as tackling the programme of the regulation of Wall Street. Wise or unwise, consistent or inconsistent, the common element in all these measures has been that of an enormous increase in the amount of Government activity and control in economic affairs.

In the specifically labour field the Federal Government has set up a comprehensive system of compulsory and contributory old age pensions; and, under national pressure, unemployment insurance has been instituted by every State in the Union. Both these innovations have already been sustained by the Supreme Court, which has also decided in the interim that minimum wage legislation by the States falls within the bounds of constitutionality. Moreover, wages, hours, and the employment of children were all regulated federally under the N.R.A., and will be regulated federally again, at least for an extremely broad definition of inter-State commerce, in case of the passage of the Administration's Wages-and-Hours Bill which has been voted by the Senate and is now under consideration in the House. Parenthetically it may be added that the 40-hour week, which first became general practice under N.R.A. regulations, has remained the prevailing, though not universal, custom of American industry even during the period without legal enforcement.

Finally, the Labour Relations Act of 1935 has reaffirmed and made still more definite the N.R.A. policy in the bitterly contested field of union organization. With the National Labour Relations Board as its enforcement agency, and with favourable decisions of the Supreme Court behind it, this legislation affirms the right of the workers to freedom of 'self-organization,' specifically outlaws employer support of 'company unions,' forbids the employer to discriminate against workers for union activity and to engage in a number of similar 'unfair labour practices' and even attempts to lay upon him the affirmative duty to bargain collectively with the chosen representatives of his workers. Nor are these only words. There is no doubt that in many

E*

cases this changed attitude of government has made the difference between the winning and the losing of strikes. It is indeed at this point that the new Government policy and the new position of organized labour are most clearly seen as a part of the same major change.

If these are the outlines of the change, what can be said of its magnitude? Two things, I think. The first is that from a European viewpoint the so-called 'Roosevelt revolution' can hardly be described as revolutionary. Though there are parts of the New Deal programme whose boldness of sweep and ingenuity of invention might well repay even more European study than they have received, it is obvious that others represent merely the belated adoption in the United States of measures long since commonplace on this side of the water. A quarter of a century after Great Britain instituted a national system of unemployment insurance, we cannot expect the world to be electrified by the announcement that the United States had at last followed suit. Again, it might be suggested that the real significance of the automobile strikes of the current year was to place the organization of the unskilled worker in something like the position that the London dock strike put it in Great Britain almost fifty years ago. Indeed, to those of you who come from a country in which union recognition and collective bargaining have long been parts of an accepted tradition, it is all but impossible to convey the sense of incredulity and outrage with which many an American employer has faced the necessity of dealing with union leaders. This, then, is the second point. However the changes may look to foreign eyes, they do represent a very great shift for individualistic America,— for a country in which self-help has been so much the traditional slogan and in which, as Sombart put it long ago, 'On roast beef and apple pie all socialistic theories die.'

iv. *Are the Recent Changes Temporary or Permanent?*

This brings me, then, to the question which I am most anxious to discuss with you and on which I am most eager to have your judgment—Are these innovations likely to be temporary or permanent? Is the new American orientation a transitory thing, born of a brief emergency and likely to die with it, or does it represent a permanent change in the life and temper of the people?

Any answer must be frankly speculative. The *Journal de Genève* took occasion last week to comment on the changeableness of United States Government policy. The point deserves examination. In my description I have, for the most part, deliberately disregarded the processes by which the changes have been brought about, and concentrated instead on the net position attained. But certainly the track by which it was reached has been a zig-zag one, marked on the one hand by sharp Administration set-backs, in the Court decisions overthrowing the N.R.A. and the A.A.A., and more recently in the defeat of the plan for drastic reform of the Supreme Court, and on the other hand by equally sudden advances, as the forces of labour and the Administration have pressed forward into new fields of action. It would, therefore, be absurd to rule out the possibility of future reversals, and there is much to be said for the suggestion that the innovations in policy have been temporary expedients, devised and accepted in great emergency but repugnant to the American tradition and unlikely to maintain themselves when the crisis is over. A number of the measures and a number of the new administrative agencies carried in their titles the word 'emergency.' Some have already been abandoned, now that the emergency is thought to be past. Certainly the New Deal found its occasion and its opportunity in the worst depression that the country and the world had ever known. No less certainly, the great majority of American business men have forgotten the eagerness with which they begged for Government intervention in the dark days of 1933. With the degree of recovery described by Professor Condliffe,[1] with Wall Street again a centre of at least mild speculative excitement, most of the business community now demands that new-fangled experiments be dropped and particularly that employers be left free to manage their own affairs. In spite of the overwhelming majority given to the President in last year's election, it is not inconceivable that the American people may before long, in the slogan adopted after an earlier period of emergency and idealism, make their way 'back to normalcy.'

Perhaps we shall. But let me suggest two grounds for doubting the conclusion. The first is an immediate and practical one. For better or worse, some of the specific things done will be hard to undo. Once the unemployed have learned to rely on the Federal Government for relief, it will be hard to persuade them, when need grows again, that the nature of the American system prevents it. It would be a rash Administration which abolished unemployment benefits and old age pensions after large masses of the people had become accustomed to receiving them. Nor will the farmers be easier to win back to *laisser-faire*.

The second doubt is more fundamental. If one looked

[1] See pages 97 to 115.

about the world in the 'twenties, it was—I believe—
American individualism that needed rather more explanation than the diverse measures of social control in other
parts of the world. Nor was this all a matter of 'roast
beef and apple pie.' Of course the material standard of
life in a country of uncrowded population and great natural
resources was in general higher than that of the old world.
But so it was in other new countries, such as Australia and
New Zealand, and as everyone knows, their abundance of
roast mutton had not served to prevent the growth of large
and powerful labour movements, or the adoption of far-
reaching measures of social control.

The American employer did not owe the extraordinary
freedom and the extraordinary prestige he enjoyed merely
to the brilliance of the technical achievements of the industry
which he controlled or to his own ingenious measures of
personnel administration. He also profited by certain
tactical advantages that were deeply rooted both in the
traditions and in the composition of the American people.
Of these traditions the most persistent has been that of
individual self-advancement. This is in part a heritage
of frontier democracy. For nearly three centuries, American
life, as our greatest historian, Turner, has pointed out, was
conditioned by the presence of free land and the opportunity of expansion to the west. Unlike the Australian
frontier of great sheep stations, or the Argentinian frontier
of great cattle ranches, the American frontier was pre-
dominantly a small man's frontier of individual, independent
farmsteads. We were a nation of homesteaders; to this
fact many of our characteristic attitudes can still be traced.

When industry arose in a country with this background,
the prevailing democratic tradition made it relatively easy

for ambitious workmen to rise to the head of the new enterprises. Thus the familiar American epic of the self-made man. Moreover, the extraordinary rate of expansion of American industry created new managerial positions fast enough so that a really appreciable number of the more energetic workmen—perhaps the very ones who might otherwise have made the most aggressive trade union leaders —could in fact hope for and secure promotion.

But the almost unchallenged domination of the individualistic ideal has rested also upon the fact that so much of the labour in American industry has been performed by recent immigrants of diverse origins. The greatest flood of the so-called 'New Immigration' from the countries of Southern and Eastern Europe began to arrive just as the westward movement came to its close and just as the rise of industry on the grand scale might perhaps have been expected to lead to the development of mass unionism. Like their predecessors before them, these newcomers came to America primarily because of their poverty and from levels of living which made American wages ,at first seem princely. It is not hard, therefore, to see the difficulties which their presence put in the way of the effective organization of a labour movement. Consider the single question of languages. Americans, myself included, are notoriously bad linguists, but I did not have to come to Geneva to have my first experience in the problem of public meetings in a number of tongues. I have been in a hall in Johnstown, Pennsylvania, crowded with striking coal miners, who sat through speeches in four languages waiting patiently for a fifth of their own, and I have seen the problem solved on a broad hillside on which the stumps of six trees held six organizers orating simultaneously each in a different language. If to this obvious confusion of tongues are added all the suspicions and prejudices of native against foreigner, and of each new race against the other, it is not hard to see why American labour has been slow in developing a coherent unity.

Thus it was partly for lack of effective challenge from below that the old attitudes persisted. It has been pointed out that the American individualism of the 1820's rested in large part on the sturdy independence of the frontiersman. I believe it is no less accurate to say that the American individualism of the 1920's rested in a considerable part on the helpless dependence of the newly arrived foreigner.

v. *Will Individualism Return ?*

If, then, we are attempting to assess the probabilities of a return to individualism, let us look at each of these factors in turn, and see in what direction they seem to have been changing. The prestige of the great business leader has been dimmed by the long depression. Too many people have learned in the meanwhile to look instead to the Government official or even to the labour leader. This effect may be temporary; it certainly has been definite. As for the influence of the frontier, it had long since been waning, in spite of its clingstone qualities. There is nothing to revive it, and an urban and industrial nation cannot be expected to retain for ever the philosophy and attitudes of an aggregation of isolated farmers. It still surprises Americans somewhat when a popular historian remarks, 'We are a nation of employees'—as if an industrial country could be anything else—but we come gradually to admit its truth. As for the career open to talents, it is doubtless still more free than in many countries. Nevertheless, many factors operate to close the doors and limit the opportunities for the self-made man. Industry's slower rate of expansion limits the creation of new openings at the top, and for those positions the greater emphasis now being laid in every line upon expensive specialized training gives more and more advantage to those who start with at least a modest amount of inherited means. It should thus be somewhat harder than before to persuade the ordinary young clerk or machine operative that the land is one of equal opportunity for individual advancement.

As for the factor of the melting-pot, the changes have been even more striking. The cumulative effects of the stoppage of immigration during the Great War and great depression, and of the limited volume of immigration following the restrictions of the early 'twenties, have brought about a most significant change in the American labour scene. There are now no longer great masses of unassimilated immigrants, though their places have in part been taken and the effect has been partly negated by the migration of Mexicans and of Negroes and poor Whites from the South. For the first time in many decades the masses even of unskilled labour in American industry are Americans —Americans, whatever their race, in the decisive sense that they have been brought up together in the same public schools. It may perhaps be this factor that has accounted for the new determination shown in certain recent strikes ; it is not unreasonable to suppose that their demands upon industry may be harder to meet than those of their inarticulate predecessors.

vi. *Conclusions.*

On each of these points, therefore, the drift of the times appears to be away from the old dominance of the individualistic ideal, and it is these factors which determine my choice between the two theories that have been suggested. It may be granted at once that the New Deal represents to a large degree a set of hasty, often extemporized, sometimes confused responses to a great emergency. No one could claim that it has produced a complete and logical body of social legislation adequate to the permanent needs of modern life. I cannot, however, take the view that its measures may therefore be quickly and thankfully abandoned with the return of at least temporary prosperity. Historically the process seems to me rather to be interpreted as the sudden forcing of a growth, some of it long overdue, which would sooner or later have occurred in any case. Doubtless there will be reaction against particular measures, and certainly the ebb and flow of battle is more to be expected than steady and orderly movement in a given direction. I should not like to be understood as prophesying the outcome of either the next strike or the next election. But a prediction which I do venture is that in two major respects the events of the last few years have indicated the broad lines of probable future development. I do not believe that the bulk of American workers will be permanently content without union organization, and I do not believe that future Governments of the United States will be able to avoid taking affirmative action in the fields in which the New Deal has pioneered.

CHAPTER VIII

HOW MAY LEAGUE PRINCIPLES BE MADE
POLITICAL REALITIES ?

by
Sɪʀ NORMAN ANGELL
Author and Publicist, Recipient of the Nobel Peace Prize, 1933

THE League is, after all, a means to an end, not an end
in itself. The ultimate end is the prevention of war
by the creation of a nascent world constitution. That constitution can be built up and the ultimate purpose of the
League fulfilled by roads other than those travelled immediately after the War under the guidance of President Wilson
—the road, that is, of calling together sixty nations and
attempting to secure agreement on a somewhat long and
complicated document. It is indeed not by that method
that some of the most useful and workable national con-
stitutions have been built up. What I am mainly concerned with today is to enquire what is the line of least
resistance to some equivalent gradual building up of an
effective and workable world constitution.

I use that word in its broadest and largest sense mainly
as meaning the effective operation of rules of the road, a
traffic code which will enable the .nations to travel the
common high road with the fear of collision and smash
reduced to the minimum.

i. *Goodwill and Common Sense are not Enough.*

First, let us be clear as to why rules of the road, some sort of constitution, are necessary at all. Why, in other words, the international anarchy cannot be made workable.

This last enquiry happens to be very timely, for behind the present efforts to create once more a Four-Power Pact is, I think, in part at least, the assumption that the old method of international relationships, without very definite or known rules of conduct, is quite compatible with peace if there is goodwill. Indeed, those who deal with international affairs might be divided broadly into two groups: those who believe that it is necessary to end the anarchy, to introduce some constitution however rudimentary, and those who believe that anarchy can be made workable by day-to-day adjustments, by the exercise of goodwill and common sense.

This latter group naturally attach great importance to the factors of conciliation and friendliness. In the Abyssinian crisis they took the view that it was more important to refrain from irritating Italy than to vindicate the League, the nascent international constitution.

If we are to be able to weigh the issues here involved, we must realize clearly in what manner anarchy, the absence of law or Government, leads to conflict.

The first purpose of any State, as of any other living organism, is self-preservation—defence. In a condition of anarchy each must be his own defender. There being no organized society, the defence of the individual cannot rest upon the power of the community; there is indeed no community properly speaking. But for an individual to be adequately defended by means of his own power, he must be stronger than any likely to attack him. Then what becomes of the defence of the weaker? Each cannot be stronger than the other. General defence becomes therefore a physical impossibility. There must be an irregular oscillation, first to one side then to the other.

Before the War we feared the power of Germany, arguing that if she, through her strategic position and her alliances, became much stronger she would be so preponderant as to deprive us of all means of defending ourselves, of defending, that is, not merely territory, but rights, interests. This was not a position we felt able to accept. Our alternative was that Germany should occupy that position of inferior power. To prove that she could do so safely, that, in other words, she need not fear our preponderant power, we used such preponderance when we possessed it at the Peace to impose the Treaty of Versailles. Looking at it today, Germany reflects that it illustrates the result of being weaker than your enemy. She is now determined to be stronger. When she is she will perhaps gradually, if necessary by war, create an entirely new treaty under which we shall be in one form or another one of the victims. We shall then do what the Germans are now doing. Build up our power to repudiate it, impose by that power a third treaty still less favourable than the first; *ad infinitum.*

This is not an imaginary situation. It represents broadly the see-saw of the inevitable contest for power, when power is the instrument by which one party to a dispute claims the right to impose its own sovereign judgment on the other party. The alternative to the dilemma is clear enough. Neither party must claim the sovereign right to be sole judge of the other, both must accept the rule of some sort of law, and the strength of the community must be pledged for the support of that law.

ii. *Mutual Defence against War.*

The one law to which common support must first of all be pledged is, of course, the law that there shall be no more war, that armed violence against any one member of a community shall be regarded as threatening the security of all the others. This very rudimentary law, the right of defence from violence, would, if a political reality, achieve the objective of abolishing war, and to that extent achieve the defence of each State.

The principle upon which it rests and without which it cannot exist at all is, however, the principle least recognized by public opinion as indispensable. Unless we are prepared to defend others, it is a physical impossibility to defend ourselves. Unless law is protective it is not worth defending, and will not be defended and will not gain power. This truth that we must defend others if we would defend ourselves is not only not recognized, it is the most usually repudiated of all the aspects of the collective system, repudiated by large sections of the Right as well as by large sections of the Left. Yet it is sufficiently obvious. Imagine a situation—which happens to exist—of, say, half a dozen lesser States whose 'defence potential' is represented by the index figure fifty, each flanked by a greater power whose 'defence potential' is represented by the index figure 100. If each of the lesser States says: 'We will only fight for ourselves, and refuse to interfere in the quarrels of others,' those States are, of course, at the complete mercy of the more powerful. But from the moment that each of the lesser States says: 'Since our defence must be collective, we shall regard an attack on one as an attack on all,' their defensive power has risen from 50 to 300, and they are in a position to resist the greater power. (I do not imply, of course, that the thing works with that mathematical simplicity. A hundred modifying factors may well enter into any such situation, but the principle remains valid in practical application as well as in theory.)

The truth has indeed received that qualified and some-what muddled recognition which is so much in our English habit. At long last we have applied it to France, with a definiteness that it has never before received. We have enunciated the principle that an attack on France or Belgium is an attack on us. That undertaking is now so unequivocal, has been so often repeated, that our hands are indeed tied in the event of France being attacked. Assume that we have to implement the promise and find ourselves, as we found ourselves in the years 1914–18, resisting a great onslaught sweeping dangerously towards the Channel coasts; in a situation, that is, far more precarious than that which faced us in the Great War, for we should almost certainly not have on our side Powers that were then our allies, and would quite probably face erstwhile allies as enemies.

Let us project ourselves forward in imagination to that situation and, having done so, answer this question: When we thus face, not aided as we were in the last war by Russia, Italy, Japan and the United States, vast hostile forces, whether on the soil of France, or on the sea, or in the air, and there is offered to us in that extremity the help of potentially the greatest military power in the world, should we refuse or accept the offer?

In other words, are we to have the help of Russia (to say nothing of Poland, Czechoslovakia and certain other States) in meeting the next attack upon France? When the situation of appalling jeopardy I have suggested has actually arisen, refusal of the aid of Russia or the other States would be regarded by our people as the act of madmen or of traitors; or of reactionaries anxious to see the democracies of the Empire and of France overcome and replaced by totalitarian systems.

Very many who at this moment boggle at 'Eastern Commitments' argue that we should allow the situation to arise before seeking the co-operation of Eastern allies in our common defence. It would be too late. Too late, that is, to deter the aggressor, to prevent war, which once it comes makes 'defence' a tragic mockery.

More than one statesman concerned with the Great War has answered the question: 'Could the War have been prevented?' by replying that it would have been prevented if Germany had foreseen that she would have to meet the forces which she did meet. The vast power finally arrayed against her was impotent to deter her for the childishly simple reason that she did not know it would be used against her.

Are we to repeat that tragedy by allowing it to be supposed that we shall look on unmoved while allies indispensable to our own defence are destroyed in detail?

The ultimate factor in effective national defence is, after all, political: Who, when the guns begin to go off, is going to be with you and who against you? That is a political not a military question.

Until we can at least provisionally and hypothetically answer it we can never know whether our armament is adequate or not. A degree of armament that would be effective in one political situation, when, say, the prospective enemy is a single State and we have powerful allies, would be quite inadequate in another situation in which we might have to meet a combination of powerful States single-handed.

It is this fact which condemns isolationism as an effective defensive policy. Suppose you assume provisionally that X is the hypothetical enemy against whom we are arming. To be in a position to keep our end up we need a given degree of armament. We get it, establish parity. X then makes an alliance which doubles his power. Parity has disappeared. What do we do? Double our armaments? Perhaps. Then the hostile Dual Alliance becomes a triple alliance. What do we do then? We make an alliance and that is the end of isolationism.

An alliance is a source of power like the air arm or the submarine. If the other side adopts it we too must do so or drop out of the race, accept a position of inferiority of power which makes defence physically impossible.

In all this discussion there is usually a confusion between obligation and liability; a quite unwarranted assumption that we increase our liabilities when we increase our obligations. We may well diminish the former by increasing the latter. An insurance company does not necessarily weaken its position by adding to its clients.

We had no obligation in respect of Serbia before the War, but we were soon to discover that we had liabilities. The liabilities would have been far less deadly if we had had clear and defined obligations which would have constituted a warning to the aggressor. That lesson, too, is probably unlearned.

The public discussion of the problem of defence is marked by a curious quality. Certain assumptions commonly made as self-evident truths are, when examined, seen to be complete fallacies, inconsistent alike with logic and with the concrete facts of experience and history.

The commonest, perhaps, and the one which dominates national thought at the moment on the subject of defence, is that possession of great national power will of itself deter aggression.

We know by the proof of recent tragic events that that is not true.

In the last War we and our Allies possessed not merely great power but power very much greater than we can perhaps ever hope to possess again. For we had on our side the power of Russia, Japan, Italy, the United States. We can be reasonably sure that not all of those will be on our side again, that some will be opposed to us. Yet we know that that power, which we can never exceed, or even duplicate, did not deter aggression.

The reason, as we have already seen, is startlingly simple: The potential aggressor did not know beforehand that these vast forces would be used against him. In the absence of this pre-knowledge, power, however great, obviously cannot deter. It serves no purpose to make punishment ferocious, if the potential criminal is unaware that the punishment exists, or if he has become convinced that it will not be applied.

Yet this first rudimentary simplicity is usually ignored or denied in discussion of the problem of defence. 'If only,' said an American admiral a few years since to me, 'our navy had been twice what it was in 1914, the Germans would never have dared to go to war.' I asked him to explain how and why, since in 1914 no German and no American could have foreseen that great American armies would cross the Atlantic to fight Germany, nor that the United States, which had fought one war against Britain over the question of sea rights (and been near to several more) would suddenly turn round and support the British view. If, at the beginning of the century, the United States had begun to build up great naval power, it is not Germany that would have been disturbed, but Great Britain, remembering always that the sea conflicts of the past have been between Britain and the United States far more than between America and Germany. About the year 1900 the German advocates of great naval power would have rejoiced to see Britain and America getting into a great naval building race. Such competition between Britain and America would not have deterred any aggressive intention that Germany might have possessed.

People say: 'Our arms are simply to resist attack.' But what is attack? Invasion? But we were not invaded in the last War; Italy was not invaded; Roumania was not invaded; Japan was not invaded; the United States was not invaded. But they all fought Germany. We have not been invaded since the Norman Conquest, but we have fought many wars.

You may say: 'Instead of threatening to meet German policy by force we should have made an attempt to redress her grievances. But she had no grievances that she could formulate. She was not then suffering under a Versailles Treaty; possessed not only all her colonies, but immense territories in Europe as well that she does not now possess.

There was no specific cause of quarrel between Germany and ourselves in 1914. Historians have often testified to the fact that our relations were freer from differences like Morocco and the Bagdad Railway than they had been for years. Yet we went to war, and if the historians are right, we went to war because Germany did not know what the Allies would regard as attack, did not know, that is, that a certain line would bring all those powers into the field against her. For when Mr. Lloyd George and other statesmen tell us that there would have been no war if certain States that ultimately did fight had said beforehand they would, it is only another way of saying that certain of the Allies, including ourselves, had not said clearly what we should regard as attack.

iii. *A Practical Policy: the Grand Alliance.*

It is often argued: 'To get peace satisfy legitimate grievance.' But there is one legitimate grievance which nations regard as more vital, more imperative, than all the rest put together—namely, lack of security. It is that grievance which explained the Great War. Germany challenged Russia because Russian predominance in Europe would, Germany feared, have deprived Germany of any adequate means of defending Germany's rights in Europe and the world. We took position against Germany because, in the last analysis, if Germany won the war she would be so much more powerful than we, or our Allies, that we should be without defence. Are we prepared to do today what we were not prepared to do in 1914, namely, see another State in Europe so predominant that we are at its absolute mercy, compelled to do its bidding, surrender territory or what not, because we are simply unable to resist?

The old method of defence failed because under it each demands rights he denies to the other: first, the right of defence by superiority of power which he denies to the weaker; second, the right of judgment he denies to the other party to the dispute. Of course the other party only accepts as long as he is compelled to. We don't cease to be aggressive merely by not going to war.

We control, or foreigners, like a good many British, think we control, about a quarter of the earth's surface. Suppose we said in effect to the world:

We are for peace. We own about a quarter of the world. We propose to close it to the rest of the world, to their trade, their emigrants, their surplus populations because it belongs to us. Its trade, its raw materials, its economic opportunities shall be exclusively under our control for our benefit. Our preponderant arms defend these claims, this *status quo*. You have no rights in this quarter of the earth except in so far as we care to grant them. The purpose of our arms is to see that you do not disturb this *status quo*, to see that you keep out and, if necessary to that end, starve without troubling us. We stand for peace.

That of course would be an extreme position. Possibly not even Lord Beavermere stands for it completely. Quite a number of our imperialists are in favour of giving away other people's colonies in order to alleviate our difficulties with importunate foreigners.

Germany has grievances, alleged difficulty of access to

raw materials, etc. Let us then frame a policy along these lines.

First, say to Germany: 'Let us have the facts about raw materials and the rest. A Fact-Finding Commission, not to make proposals but simply to establish the facts as to whether you are at a disadvantage in the matter of buying raw materials. If the facts show that you are, we stand ready to correct the inequality. Will you help in the impartial establishment of the facts and then publish the findings broadcast among your people?

Second, in view of the fact that what people on one side of a frontier regard as grossly unjust people on the other regard as obviously fair, will you in such cases either accept the principle of umpire or undertake not to disturb the *status quo* by war? For correcting injustices by war means making the more powerful party the judge and getting a worse *status quo* than ever.

Third, since nearly the whole case of the principal Have-Not States is that the *status quo* becomes with the passage of time inequitable, will they agree to the creation of institutions or organs of peaceful change and co-operate in their functions?

Fourth, we should make it clear that we form with other States accepting those principles a defensive alliance or confederation based on the principles that an attack on one is an attack on all. Such an alliance, we should point out, is not 'encirclement,' because membership is open to all on equal terms; we offer to others the precise principle of defence we claim for ourselves. (The nucleus of such an alliance would be Britain, France, Russia, Czechoslovakia, drawing in later Poland, Jugoslavia, Roumania.)

If the Have-Not States co-operate on those terms, we

have recreated the League. If they do not co-operate, it is still more necessary to maintain that confederation among as many allies as we can obtain. For arms, allies and commitments we shall have in any case. It is better that the alliance should make an acceptable offer to 'the other side,' than merely create a competitive combination which neglects to make any provision for the security of others, who would otherwise regard it as a threat to themselves.

The probability is, of course, that as soon as our political commitments have no longer a 'League' connotation, no longer a 'Geneva flavour,' conservative opposition will fall away. The assumption seems to be that commitment on behalf of 'the League' is commitment for some vague and dangerous altruistic purpose remote from British interest; but that commitments of the old kind, like those which involved us in 1914, are on behalf of definite British interest; are 'realist' where the Geneva arrangements are 'sentimental'; that the old alliances were safe and protective; the Geneva alliances dangerous and aggressive.

If, by calling the political principle of collective defence, which underlies the League's effort, by some other name, we can secure the adhesion of the enemies of 'sentiment' (who fear words so much more than the things which they express), there is, of course, a good deal to be said for changing the name.

If in the course of the next few years the Grand Alliance, which seems now in process of formation, stands mainly for the principles outlined; if it makes it clear that it guarantees, not frontiers but peace; that the significance of frontiers may be greatly modified by voluntary agreements; that the chances of real and lasting change are better in that direction than by the hazards of war, then we may create a situation in which it will gradually become plain to the German and Italian peoples (and Governments) that for them to continue outside the combination would involve more risks and less power than they would possess as members of the club.

CHAPTER IX

PEACEFUL CHANGE: AN ANALYSIS OF SOME CURRENT PROPOSALS

by

MALCOLM W. DAVIS

Associate Director, European Centre, Division of Intercourse and Education, Carnegie Endowment for International Peace

i. *The Meaning of Peaceful Change.*

'PEACEFUL Change' has always seemed, to my mind, a bad phrase for the subject in view— a bad phrase although a brilliant one, and perhaps bad because brilliant enough to be a bit dazzling and so to hide the meaning of the question that it suggests. It appears to imply that changes, readjustments between States, can and should take place, as a matter of course, peaceably and quietly. In fact, when one comes down to the essential examination of the problem, one finds that, like the possibility of readjustment by war, it is also fundamentally a matter of power and of welfare. What is involved basically is rather 'Safe Change' or 'Change with Security'—and consequently 'exchange' as well as 'change' —for unless satisfied people can feel that they gain as well as give something they value, and that they retain safety in doing so, then they are as likely to resist a settlement even to the point of violence as dissatisfied people are to insist by the threat or use of violence if they can. So the topic of 'Peaceful Change' is here presented in the sense of 'Change with Security.'

146

ii. *Where and How Changes have become Necessary.*

First of all, an inquiry is necessary: Why are we considering the subject to-day? How has it come to be a concern of immediate interest now? The grievances related to it have been with us ever since the World War, and some of the deeper-lying ones longer still. Many of them have grown acute particularly since the crisis which began in 1929–30 and the depression in economic life throughout the world. Nevertheless, 'Peaceful Change' has only become a theme for active and continued discussion during the past two or three years.

What has occurred? In order to understand, one must go back a little in history and briefly recall certain events. In doing so, the intention will be in a scientific spirit so to state things that they can be recognized as true whether one likes it or not, to define facts, disregarding partisan preferences.

Twenty years ago American entry for the first time into a conflict on the continent of Europe altered the balance of power and created a new order of political problems. Leaving aside all discussion of what might have happened otherwise, two conclusions are certain: First, obviously the peace settlement—whatever its terms—would have been a different one and the division of Europe and European possessions would not have been what it is. Second, and more significant since it was the condition determining the peace settlement, it is highly improbable that except for the intervention of the United States either European group of nations at war could have imposed the disarmament of the other and the demilitarization of its territories and held it powerless. Force from outside made that possible, and the result was a situation without precedent.

Americans generally showed little sign of realizing what they had done or of having wished to do exactly that. Discontented with the experience as a whole, they tended to turn away from Europe and to withdraw to their own continental position between the two oceans. Effective refusal by the United States to consent to ratification of the peace treaties or to join the League of Nations—once again, whatever one may think about it—none the less left another situation sure: it left the Allied Powers, and in particular England and France, in a position to control the course of European events and to direct major policy, so long as they agreed with each other on the main points in practice and principle.

This held true down to as recent a time as two or three years ago, despite differences over policy in one episode or another between Governments at London and Paris. Then indications of deep divergency in the tendencies of their thought began to multiply. These came to a culminating point following the Anglo-German Naval Treaty, negotiated separately, which roused French resentment, and the conversations between the Cabinet chiefs and diplomats of Paris and Rome with the result seemingly of a Franco-Italian tacit understanding in regard both to Mediterranean relations and interests in Africa, especially in Ethiopia. Amid these complications came the German declaration of a free hand in rearmament and in army reorganization. A year later there ensued the reoccupation of the Rhineland by surprise tactics, and consequently its remilitarization as a frontier. Since then we have experienced a feverish impulse to the rematching of strengths which dominates the situation to-day. Germany, in effect, has reacquired the military and naval power to have her own policy and to pursue it. To this has been added a working accord between Berlin and Rome. The outlook is full of uncertainties, in which London and Paris have drawn closer together again with a view to regaining a measure of the control that had been let slip.

Coincidently, there has developed more and more discussion about 'Peaceful Change.' It has been made evident, increasingly, that any security in the sense of freedom from the menace of possible war was at least highly questionable unless an attempt were made to open prospects of reasonable satisfaction to the claims dissatisfied and insurgent nations. The problem, then, is basically a matter of policies of power, prestige and prosperity.

iii. *Difficulties of affecting Change without War.*

Discussions on 'Collective Security' in the International Studies Conference held at London in 1935, under the auspices of the Institute of Intellectual Co-operation, led to a clear conclusion that this problem could not be satisfactorily solved without provision for reasonable reconsideration and settlement of situations threatening trouble. Otherwise, neither the dissatisfied insurgent nations nor the many neutrals, so-called, whose support for an international system would be indispensable, could be counted upon to collaborate effectively in emergencies. So it was decided to spend the succeeding two years in analysing this problem of the peaceful adjustment of disputes between States, which has come to be known as 'Peaceful Change.'

The Conference on this subject took place at Paris in June of this year; and the elements of it selected for treatment here are drawn largely from the Conference discussions and documents, of which they form only a part since it is impossible in a brief space to cover the field as a whole.

Analysis began, as has been indicated, with the idea that in order to prevent war it is necessary to provide other means of change. Yet this aspect of the problem has received least attention from the statesmen concerned first with guaranteeing security. Others have emphasized it, ineffectually in the past; but actual changes have been few and have been accomplished chiefly by agreement independently between the parties or by acquiescence in one-sided action. Change of the character implied in the problem under study, however, means not merely a bargain with freedom for the parties to modify it according to their own power and will, but rather an actual alteration in international legal methods and order including the influence and interests of other parties.

The egoism of individuals, multiplied by the mass of a nation, may ordinarily present group selfishness in the guise of patriotic sentiment. For some, this means conservation—keeping what they have, if possible—and these comprise not only the victors in the World War but also most of the neutrals. For others, it means expansion—gaining what they lost or want, if possible—and these comprise not only the vanquished but also some of the victors as well. Yet it needs to be borne constantly in mind that there is no such thing in the world as a completely 'satisfied' or a completely 'unsatisfied' State. All the popular talk about the 'haves' and the 'have-nots' is in this sense confusing and inaccurate. It misleads thought by disregarding the fact that there is always a basis of exchange, of give and take, the only peaceful solution.

A chief difficulty in the way is that within nations agreement and authority impose obedience and order in an organized society which secures the settlement of troubles. Between nations no adequate agreement or authority exists. The idea of international law for international life carries emotional force only for a few individuals, as yet. For a large majority of people it is an idea lacking fervour, a lesson to be learned, a reasoned truth without warmth. In the competition for power and prestige and profit, the aim and hope can only be gradually to link a morale of nations and a new prestige with the realization of the general interest as the genuine interest also of each people. The obstacles to that are clear enough at present.

For these reasons, changes in frontiers and territorial transfers are the hardest kind of readjustment to effect peacefully. The land of a nation is felt to be inseparably part of its peculiar right. So there is the greatest resentment over losing and the greatest resistance to giving up any of it. Readjustment in situations involving territory may be more practicable by adding new obligations in regard to them, under international rules, than by calling on one party simply to cede rights to another. A Government can more readily yield something to an international joint system in which it acts as an equal than to one rival State.

The economic road often looks the easiest to take towards understandings—particularly to Americans who desire to evade political questions in relation to the rest of the world and who tend to think that economic and financial proposals may relieve them of this worry. Nevertheless, economic schemes are found—if rigorously thought through —infallibly to lead to politics, for they concern means of military power. They do offer, however, advantages in that economic claims and concessions can be examined objectively, while the motives of policy frequently cannot, and that they generally have to bring into consideration the broader collective group interests which are parts of each problem.

In general, as to available methods for the peaceful redress of wrongs, it has to be recognized that compulsion and international legislation are not likely to be practicable soon—justifiable in logic as they may seem. Compromise and persuasion, though weaker words, express the possibilities today. That is to say, we have at hand the devices of established international law and practice—arbitration, conciliation, mediation, advisory or conclusive court opinions on provisions in treaties, commissions of inquiry into causes of dispute, the limited resources of Article 19 in the Covenant of the League of Nations, clauses in conventions providing for revision, and the developing method of conferences which, despite failures, holds out promise and has often realized results. These leave to the evolution of the future such agencies as courts of equity for judgment between nations, with obligatory observance of their pronouncements to be enforced if necessary by concerted pressure, or as an international legislative and police power.

iv. *The Population Problem.*

Now, as regards the people, who are the realities concerned in all the controversies—since States, as such, do not suffer, but it is the people who compose them that pay the penalties

for their States, as the President of the International
Studies Conference observed rightly—there has been complicated discussion among experts as to what constitutes
'optimum population' or 'over-population' or 'under-
population.' All one can clearly conclude is that there
is a distinction between nations which claim to be over-
populated and a few among them which others concede to
be over-populated, probably. Because a feeling of population pressure is one of the causes of discontent, remedies
require to be sought; and the first ones proposed are the
obvious ones of higher industrialization to provide work,
internal resettlement or external settlement in colonies or
other countries, and family limitation. There is further a
suggestion, by an expert in the International Labour Office,
of demographic planning, with agreements between Governments on means and methods for relief, on the levels of
living standards, on equality of treatment for residents,
and on general social policy, to be worked out through
an international conference and a permanent commission.
There are, evidently, the problems of the capacity of the
continents relatively to support populations, and of the
difficulties encountered in the assimilation and expatriation
of migrants, and also of barriers to emigration and immigration. Likewise, it is to be remarked that migration is
only an effective relief for population pressure if along with
it goes a limitation policy on population in the sending
State. In other words, it is not an absolute but a relative
solution, although there is agreement generally that it is
a temporary remedy for both over-population and under-
population if the rate of increase is lessening in the sending
State and if the receiving State gets the kind of people it
wants.

A modern obstacle to this solution for over-populated States is the evident fact that most former areas of colonial settlement are now countries controlling their own policies of population, and that all colonies are comprised in the systems of managing and owning Powers. The era of free occupation is over; and all the newer nations are cautious and conservative in calculating the limited numbers of people that they are prepared to receive. They emphasize firmly, moreover, objections to accepting immigrants from nations that wish their people abroad to keep their allegiance to their countries of origin rather than become citizens of their new lands; and they insist on the right of selection. In any event, their estimates do not afford an effective outlet for any over-populated States in Europe and Asia—except in the case of Brazil whose spokesmen indicate a possibility of receiving considerable numbers of agricultural labourers on plantations.

The financing of migratory movements and of enterprises for settlers is another difficulty. In connection with it there is the suggestion of an international bank controlling funds for the purpose. There is also the suggestion of an international commission, to keep in touch with all labour exchanges and so to direct migration usefully towards work and to assure equity of treatment and guard against national pressure or propaganda.

Finally, in the consideration of all the possible proposals there emerges more and more sharply the conclusion that an improvement in the economic and industrial position of the world, with a consequent increase in living standards, would afford the best comparatively rapid relief, while awaiting the longer working of readjustments in population.

v. *The Colonial Problem.*

Colonies come naturally next to mind, in connexion with demographic problems. Records show them, however, to be dubious as outlets for over-population, as they also are coming to be as fields of financial profit. Out of some nineteen million emigrants from Europe during a half-century, according to one estimate, only 500,000 are found to have settled in colonial regions.

Among the changes, falling short of actual cession of colonies which appears unlikely, that might be offered partly to satisfy nations not now owning them, there are a number of suggestions. One, brought forward by representatives of non-colonial States themselves, is participation by their nationals in the civil and expert services of colonies. Another is better or equal status for foreigners in colonies, as compared with that of nationals of the colony-owning Power. A third is facilitation of investment and of collaboration in colonial enterprises by foreigners. To investment, however, an impediment in frequent instances at the present time is restriction on the export of funds imposed by non-colonial countries themselves. A second and related difficulty is the fact that the claimant country may want any colonial commerce or enterprise included in its monetary system, instead of continuing to operate as part of the system of the proprietor State—a difficulty that emphasizes the fiscal and industrial programmes of self-sufficiency being pursued by many nations in a period of political uncertainty.

Chartered companies of a national type, acquiring concessions to develop resources or trade, constitute one remedy suggested. These might be similarly blocked, in some

F*

cases, by existing limitations on capital exports; but these restrictions in turn are due in large measure to the crisis and depression in economic and financial movements between nations, which have contributed to make colonies seem desirable as possessions within the monetary systems of the operating States.

International chartered companies, with co-operation by the monetarily poorer and richer States together, might be able better to function. This suggestion implies, obviously, co-ordination of different groups interested, control of any materials produced and of their sale and use, elimination of political purposes and emphasis on an industrial and labour programme solely. While the barriers to complete realization of such a system are numerous, progress along these lines may promise more results than along any others now.

One suggestion, namely, that there should be an agreement to give equality of access at all times to colonial sources of foodstuffs and industrial materials, reveals the strategical substance of the problem. To do so 'at all times' means not only in peace but also in war. The resistances shown to this suggestion make it evident that colony-owning Powers think of them in terms of their tactical use, as bases of operation and reserve supply, as well as in terms of their commercial importance, and for motives of safety do not desire to decrease their control in emergencies.

Another international recourse is the colonial mandate system of the League of Nations, one of the most significant and suggestive developments since the World War. First of all, it affords the advantages of care for the interests of native populations, equal economic opportunity for nationals of different States, absence of fortification or of militarization of the natives for national power purposes, and examination yearly by the non-partisan Mandates Commission into the handling of matters by the responsible State. Finally, it offers a system which might be extended, both because nothing in practice or principle excludes a non-League State from holding a mandate, and also because a non-member nation, the United States, claims and emphasizes an interest in the disposition of all mandates on the ground that by the peace settlement title to them was vested in the Allied and Associated Powers of which it was one. For the sake of satisfactory understandings, moreover, it would be easier from the point of view of prestige and psychological sentiment for a mandatory Power to acquiesce in the international transfer of supervision to another power than to cede a colony directly or to concede outright privileges by request or subject to threats. More and more colonies might conceivably be included under the mandate system voluntarily, with the aims of developing and emancipating them gradually by an international joint plan.

Once again, it must be stressed that in relation to this subject as to population problems, the conclusion from exchanges of studies and views has been that an element essential to any immediate improvement is freer general investment and loans and increasing international trade throughout the world. This is the base needed for plans of readjustment in the present situation.

vi. *Raw Materials and Markets.*

From these questions one comes to the related subject of markets and materials of production. Here the complications concentrate. For example, estimates show that the United States of America and the British Commonwealth between them control three-fourths of the industrial key mineral resources in the world. Soviet Russia comes third, the French Empire fourth, and the Netherlands Empire fifth. Furthermore, it is to be noted that colonies are more important for agricultural products than for industrial materials, excepting tin, their output being more in the fields of foodstuffs, vegetable fibres and oils, and rubber. The problem of raw materials is primarily one of access to resources in sovereign State territories. Nevertheless, the bargaining basis of give and take exists—for even the United States, although best off from the point of view of industrial production supplies, has to buy largely nickel, rubber and tin, to name only a few of its major purchases. It is not, consequently, an entirely 'satisfied' State.

Among the chief difficulties in the way of readjustments in favour of the less fortunate States are the international and national plans in force at present for restricting production and sale. These are cited by the claimants as a grievance, but opinion tends to the view that they might not prove serious if there were faith in the maintenance of peace, and if means of purchase were released by decreasing embargoes on exporting financial funds and by liberating trade as a basis of exchange. However, we are living in a period of fearing possible war and of barriers to commerce and control of monetary reserves, an armistice economy of instable production, a rearmament truce. In such a time the decline of investment and international marketing is a primary problem. A conclusion from this is that freer trade is an effective instrument of reasonable readjustment, of 'Peaceful Change.' By contrast, expectation of war leads straight to a demand to get, or a determination to hold, control of production and resources and a tendency to cut down exchanges. Restrictions on the development of national resources by foreigners, another grievance of the disadvantaged claimants, are connected directly with the expectation of war as well as with exclusive interests.

vii. *Conclusions.*

As a preface to solutions suggested, it has to be remarked that there is no prospect of the proprietor States simply handing over part of their mineral reserves to other States merely to 'satisfy' them. What has to be sought is an exchange of fair values. Chartered companies working concessions might offer a palliative, avoiding the issue of outright transfer, although they would entail complications if there were insistence on limiting them to the monetary national systems of the States obtaining concessions. International chartered companies might prove more workable, combined as they would have to be with accords controlling access, production, purchase and use. It is interesting that this suggestion has been urged by an American expert, and that to this idea from a non-League State it was French criticism which emphasized the obstacles and perils possibly presented by it. There is, further, the suggestion of opening to participants from the consuming countries the opportunity of representation on the boards of management operating the production of materials.

All these partial proposed remedies for discontent with the distribution of industrial resources, as in the cases of population pressure and of colonies, have given rise to discussions which stressed the urgency of a betterment in the economic and financial situation of the world, as an essential and first requisite. Many official and unofficial investigations and recommendations along these lines have been made in the past few years, and certain plans have already been set under way, of all of which we may in the near future learn the outcome, whether discouraging or encouraging.

Meanwhile, one may recall that in another day it was said, 'In time of peace, prepare for war,' and add that in our day—remembering the years from 1914 to 1918 and conflicts that have occurred since then—the motto needs to be, 'In time of war, prepare for peace—if you can.'

CHAPTER X

FRENCH POLICY AND THE RECONSTRUCTION OF THE LEAGUE

by

M. JACQUES KAYSER

Vice-President, Radical Socialist Party of France

SINCE the founding of the League all the French cabinets have stated their desire to support it, and in fact most of them have really given it their support. The present Government, the Government of the Popular Front, is continuing the task of the preceding Government, and in agreement with the will of the French nation, which on this point has expressed itself very clearly and very forcefully, is attempting to save the League of Nations. The League of Nations needs attention. It is in the throes of a double crisis, a political crisis and a moral crisis. The League has often on technical grounds and in many fields helped in the practical co-operation between nations. But in spite of all that the founders of the League promised and hoped, we are unfortunately obliged to recognize first, that the League, far from being a League of the peoples, has been a club for the Government leaders; secondly, that it has wasted its moral prestige and has never built up its material power; thirdly, that it has been unable to avoid the conquest of nations without self-defence, those very nations that Wilson sought to protect in creating the Covenant.

I must complete this gloomy résumé by a comparison

161

between the epoch of the armistice, an epoch freed at last from an abominable past, and the present time, which seems ruled by the promise of an abominable future.

i, *Four Conditions for Peace.*

In 1918 it was generally admitted that in order to save peace four conditions were necessary: that the nations must be directed by democratic Governments; that from the economic co-operation between nations some progress in the commercial system must arise; that disarmament must become a fact; and that the 'evil effects' of private manufacture and commerce of armaments must be 'prevented.'

In 1918, at the end of the War, the whole of Europe was under democratic rule. To-day most of the European countries are dictatorships or under a regime approaching dictatorship. During the years which followed the War Europe was tending toward the organization of international economy. In the course of recent years autarchy has been triumphant, and the total sum of international commerce has been sinking at an alarming speed. Until the Disarmament Conference was opened there was some hope that a convention for the limitation of armaments would be reached. Since 1932 the armaments race has again begun. During fifteen years measures were proposed in vain against the private manufacture and sale of armaments. Nowhere but in France, by the law of nationalization of armaments, has anything been accomplished. We must then say that on these four points vital for the peace of Europe—democracy, economic co-operation, disarmament, and abolition of the private manufacture of armaments—there has been the contrary of progress. How then can we recognize anything but the failure of the League? But we must seek out the reasons of this failure. Wherein lies the fault?

There is no doubt always danger of making mistakes if one tries to seek out the causes of things too scientifically or rationally, and I remember a story that my great friend, M. Herriot, told me some time ago, a story which illustrates this danger very forcefully. There was once a drinker who every time he came home drunk was sorely beaten up by his wife. Very much annoyed by that treatment, he decided to put an end to his drinking and, being of a rational turn of mind, he attempted to discover what drink it was that could have so evil an effect on his spirits. The first night he drank whisky and soda, came home drunk and his wife beat him. The second night he tried Scotch and soda, came home drunk and his wife beat him. The third night he took brandy and soda, came home drunk and his wife beat him again. 'Eureka,' then cried the drinker, 'it must be the soda!' This story has a parallel. The enemies of the League have a manner of reasoning which seems very like to that of the drinker in the story. In the Manchukuo affair they said: 'In this troublesome case we see Japan, but here too is the Covenant of the League. In the Rhineland affair they said: 'The peace of Europe is at stake; here is Germany, but here again is the Covenant of the League. In the Ethiopian affair they said: 'Here is a new conflict. On one side Italy, and once more the Covenant of the League.' And they concluded, 'Every time we see trouble somewhere we find the League implied. We are obliged, therefore, to conclude that: It must be the League.'

Now the truth is that the responsibility for failure belongs more to the Governments than to the League itself. If these Governments had remained faithful to the motto which some of them had chosen, and against which none of them had dared to protest, 'The Covenant, the whole Covenant, nothing but the Covenant,' certainly much trouble would have been avoided.

Let us take the case of the Italo-Ethiopian conflict. There might be some discussion as to whether or not Ethiopia should have been admitted to the League, but from the moment that the League of Nations had been confronted with the question, from the moment that a study of the conflict had been considered by the League, it was the League's duty to apply the Covenant. To the nations Members of the League, the League offered the resources of the Covenant. What more could it do? The nations Members of the League, and first among them France and Great Britain, did not apply the Covenant. They discussed, adjourned, negotiated, and preferred to apply only partially those rules whose strength resides mainly in their indivisability.

I state as a fact that if at the start M. Mussolini had known the Covenant would be fully applied, he would have accepted the pacific offers made in August and in September. I state as a fact that as soon as the first acts of war had been accomplished by Italy, if Italy had been stricken by all the economic sanctions of which the League members disposed, she could not have pursued this adventure. It was not the League as a pacific instrument but certain Governments which showed weakness in applying sanctions. Let us speak henceforward of failure of certain Governments rather than of failure of the League.

That is why we do not admit that our hopes have been in vain. If we are obliged to recognize the failure of this League, we remain faithful to our ceaseless demand for the rebuilding of the real League of Nations.

But if the League is to live, the delegates at Geneva must have the League spirit. They must understand the real meaning of international co-operation. They must consider the League as an instrument which does not only work one way; from which they expect direct advantages, but which they abandon when it calls for sacrifices in conflicts which do not touch them closely. On many other points we seek in vain for the Geneva spirit. The Geneva spirit implied a direct association of nations. The Covenant was to be the universal law. The Covenant was to forbid or render null all agreements *inter se* contrary to the terms of the Covenant. The will was clearly to oppose the ideal of one single universal agreement to the system of localized individual bonds. The reserve formulated in Article 21 on the treaties of arbitration and the regional understandings is a clear proof of this desire.

For many reasons, however, and especially because of the failure to make the Covenant precise in its universal framework, a multitude of regional agreements and treaties of a local and limited character has arisen. Although many of these remain open to other signatures, they are not completely in accordance with the spirit of the League. The League of Nations is no longer exclusive or even the main link in the association of nations. The nations have become bound by agreements narrower and more direct.

In 1919 it was understood that widespread disarmament must take place in order to enable the League to work normally and fulfil its promise. Here, again, the League cannot be blamed. The promises contained in the Covenant were workable. The nations never made a serious and unselfish effort in order that they might be applied, and the whole organization conceived on a background of disarmament, or at least a low limitation of armament, could no longer work normally and profitably, since it was checked by the growth of the armaments race between nations.

Finally, the authors of the Covenant believed that an association of nations, which meant the willing allegiance of nations to a single international law, was possible only if it was founded with the help of nations whose regime reposed on co-operation and respect of the law. In other words, only Governments under democratic control could usefully co-operate in a League, because these Governments alone would be moved by a spirit of mutual assistance, because these Governments alone would recognize that above national sovereignty there exists the higher sovereignty of international law.

We should then be tempted to declare: Yes, we remain faithful to the League. We have not lost the will to see the League fulfil its promise, that is, to function completely and under all the conditions necessary for its very existence: democratic Governments, disarmament, abolition of all agreements *inter se* contrary to the word of the Covenant. Unfortunately, it is clear that for the present we cannot expect to see these conditions fulfilled. But is that a reason to lose hope?

Must we give up the fight and sacrifice a weak but living international organization because we have not been able to make it perfect? We must certainly strive to create a perfect League. But we serve peace also if we save that League which exists, if we adapt the League to present conditions, if we modify and better the League so that it may still be of use.

ii. *Some Current Criticisms.*

Let us draw up a list of practical criticisms addressed to the League. First, that the League exists only in order to maintain the territorial status which is a result of evil peace treaties. Secondly, that the League is paralysed by the unanimity rule. Thirdly, that in the discussion of subjects which are of vital importance to Europe the League associates far away countries, which intervene only to place vetoes which have been suggested to them by nations which are directly interested, but cannot take openly the responsibility of such opposition. Finally, the last objection is that the Great Powers have not the influence which their importance implies, and also that the small nations are backed into positions which their national dignity cannot tolerate. Let us examine each one of these criticisms.

The League was not created in order to maintain the *status quo.* If Article 10 guarantees the 'territorial integrity' of all its members, it is closely linked with Article 19 which provides for the possibility of examining a 'reconsideration of treaties which have become inapplicable.' The League thus contains the legal possibility of pacific reconsideration of treaties. In that famous letter of June 16, 1919, to the leader of the German delegation to the Peace Conference, M. Clemenceau admits that. He writes, 'The treaty creates . . . the organism necessary . . . to find the means to modify from time to time, the rule of 1919, in order to adapt it to new facts and to new circumstances whenever these may arise.'

Never has a demand for treaty reconsideration come up before the League of Nations. It is said that this is not practical because of the necessity for a unanimous vote. Might not some action be taken without changing the unanimity rule, which would allow the proceedings to begin simply after a majority vote? But since it is often argued that the unanimity rule must be modified, let us examine exactly what is understood. It could be said that whenever 'unanimity' appears in the Covenant it means the vote excluding the parties to the dispute. Thus the voices of those parties would not be counted. In the sixth paragraph of Article 15 of the Covenant this is the method adopted.

I should like to see those methods generally extended, particularly for Article 11 which states that 'in case of war or threat of war the League can take any action that may be deemed wise and effectual to safeguard the peace of the nations.' At present the agreement of a nation which has menaced peace or started war is necessary if this action is to be taken! This paradox has been allowed to subsist. It explains the hesitations and inertia in many cases. But it is not enough to consider Article 11. I believe that in general the unanimity rule must be abolished. We are glad to see that this suggestion figures among the initiatives of the French Government.

We consider that the League of Nations must be universal, and I believe that its moral prestige and power reside in the fact that it brings together, or can bring together, the nations of the whole world with the nations of Europe. But it seems to me that it is necessary to emphasize that

the settlement of European problems should not be paralysed by the veto of South American, Asiatic or African
nations. Thus, for example, although the universality of
the League be maintained, it could be conceived that
either by abolishing the unanimity rule or by a geographical
repartition of the rights and duties of its members, the
League should be freed of the legal but unfortunate
intervention of countries that are in no way interested in
the case. On this point it seems necessary that a distinction
be drawn between the bodies which take action and those
which are charged with control.

For this reason I suggest that the safeguard of international law must lie in the hands of the community of
nations, but that the obligation of effective action must
be regionalized. The growth within the League of a
European League or of a European 'section' of the League
is an idea to which I, for my part, am not opposed. But
this must in no way hinder the growth of the universal
organization, nor destroy it. It must not become a Pan-
European movement which might some day attempt to
pitch one continent against another. On the other hand,
it seems impossible to organize peace if there is either an
extreme predominance of the Great Powers, or absolute
equality between powers whose responsibilities are world-
wide and those whose concerns are more limited.

The League must not be based on questions of hierarchy.
But there is no reason why it should not reform the composition of the Council. I do not consider as a good
method that which consists in creating new membership
whenever a Power demands it, and threatens in order to
obtain. How is it that some small States in South America
sit at the Council, whereas Holland has not sat at the

Council for a long time, and that Austria, for instance, has never been a member of the Council?

But all this may seem very abstract, and nothing would be worse than to suggest that the League is something abstract and that it thrives on abstractions only. There are before us two problems, and both dilemmas. The first: Do we need a stronger League or a weaker League? The second (and this is the classic dilemma—to be or not to be—) : Shall the League live on or shall we allow it to die? In other words, Can something be done to preserve the League, even as it is now?

iii. *The Problem of Sanctions.*

In the first dilemma we are faced with the problem of sanctions. For a weaker League is a League amputated of both assistance and sanctions, and a stronger League is a League armed with a new organization of assistance and sanctions. If there are no sanctions, we fall back fatally to the methods of pre-War diplomacy: private negotiations and more private negotiations. For what becomes of collective action without a system of sanctions? Absence of sanctions means that the aggressor is encouraged to continue his aggression. Collective action then becomes collective inaction. The conflict must then remain a local conflict, the victim of aggression is isolated and the victory goes necessarily to the aggressor. The Powers when they feel that they are under a menace are encouraged to contract limited alliances. Thus absence of sanctions means the defeat of the spirit of the League. The very condition of success for the League is abolished.

Thus the League, in order to be serviceable and effectual,

needs a sanction system. What sanctions? Economic and financial sanctions certainly, but military sanctions also. No doubt someone will object: 'Military sanctions must not be considered, for they might lead to war. They may even be confused with war.' But are we certain that economic sanctions are safely outside the path of war? I do not believe so. In a letter to *The Times* written a year ago Sir Arthur Salter used a decisive argument: 'A would-be aggressor will take a gamble. Precisely because they have been uncertain, sanctions will fail to prevent aggression and may be unable to defeat it without war on a considerable scale.' There must be, therefore, Sir Arthur Salter continues, 'a collective preponderance in strength of countries loyal to the League system over those likely to assail it.'

However, there must be no misunderstanding as to the reason for applying sanctions. I do not believe that war can be vanquished by war. I do not believe that war can be avoided by making war general and widespread. But I think that the risks of war will be lessened if war is made more certainly dangerous for the aggressor than for the victim.

The mechanism of the sanctions must be such that it contains its whole preventive power. The aggressor must know that at the very moment that the aggression takes place all the members of the League will immediately and simultaneously apply all economic and financial sanctions. Here we reach an important question: How can the aggressor be defined? On this point the definition given by M. Litvinoff at Geneva, and which figures in certain pacts of non-aggression signed between the Soviet Union and its neighbours, is entirely satisfactory and might find its place within the Covenant. I need not recall it here.

It can be found in the pacts of non-aggression concluded between the Soviet Union and her neighbours, and registered at the League of Nations. It is evident that in case of aggression a special sacrifice can be demanded of one nation only in so far as the sacrifice is shared by the community of nations. It would be entirely unjust that while accomplishing its international duty one nation should be more harshly called upon than another.

Let us beware, also, not to lead wholesome ideas astray by exaggeration. For example, military assistance must be organized regionally. A strong regional organization would, moreover, present the advantage of being more surely preventive.

Since we consider the problem of military sanctions we are obliged to face the facts: military sanctions can be of decisive utility only if the coalition of sanctionist nations has an armed force far superior to that of the aggressor. To obtain this, there is only one way: limitation of armaments. If there is no control of armaments, the aggressor will bide his time until he is certain to possess the force of arms necessary to overpower his adversaries. If there is limitation and control of armaments the risk of aggression will be lessened. The aggressor himself will understand that victory under these circumstances will be difficult to obtain.

iv. *From Competitive Armaments to Economic Co-operation.*

But dare we even dream of disarmament, or of a halt in the armaments race? Leon Blum, in his speech at Lyons last January, 1937, put forward an audacious point of view, but no answer was ever given to the propositions he made. He considered as closely bound together the question of military disarmament and the question of economic disarmament and economic co-operation. Here briefly is his plan. The nations are busy, he said, with rearmament. Rearmament gives work to the workers of the factories. If there were a halt in this rearming, unemployment would increase and raw materials would uselessly accumulate. Another outlet then must be found for the factories working for national defence. Is there a more useful way of employing men and materials than in the building up and equipment of certain distressed areas of Central Europe, Asia or Africa?

The French Premier's plan presents a twofold advantage. First, it makes possible a halt in the armaments race and prevents the ill effects of rearmament. Secondly, it conceives co-operation in the economic field.

Economic co-operation! Here again is a problem for the League to solve. Until now, no decisive steps have been taken. The League has given it attention. It has furnished statistics and offices. But here again the Governments have been unable or have not known how to make use of the League. Nothing has been usefully accomplished.

Furthermore, it seems impossible to imagine that peace may be lasting with the present partition of raw materials. Committees of experts are at work, but the problems are as yet unsolved.

I do not wish here to go deeply into these matters, for they do not fall exactly within the framework of the question I am treating. But I must indicate briefly how closely they are bound to the general problem. And I must point out that in my belief the rationalization of production and of exchange is one of the tasks to which the League owes most urgent attention.

v. *The Present Position.*

And here we are before the second dilemma. The League of Nations must keep its place and act even in an anxious and armed world. Although it be far from perfect the League can still serve peace. If we let the League be destroyed, we give up all hope of international organization.

While France demands that the League be reinforced in the way of 'automatism and of obligation,' France defends the League, imperfect as it is. Though France demands that the League be recast, France demands that those measures be taken, limited though they may be, that may immediately and certainly help to safeguard peace.

If these measures are not taken, peace will be lost. A weakened League—and the *status quo* is for the League a new degree of weakness—will lead inevitably to a new development of the race of armaments and alliances. The nations whose interests are limited rather than world-wide are taking measures against the probable shortcomings of the League. Mr. Rustu Aras, Foreign Secretary of Turkey, illustrates their fears when he demands for his country, as he did some months ago, the right to remilitarize the Straits. He writes in the official memorandum: 'The political crisis has shown clearly that the existing mechanism of collective security is too slow in coming into action, and that a tardy decision can annul the benefits of international action.'

We know that nothing lasting can be accomplished so

long as in the world, and particularly in Europe, there are dictatorships which derive their very existence from a permanent excitement of national prestige.

Let us not close our eyes before facts. We are obliged to consider things as they exist. Governments negotiate with Governments, and not with the leaders of the opposition. The rôle of diplomacy today is to maintain peace, to smooth out difficulties, to prevent incidents. And for these reasons the League must not be and is not an alliance turned against the dictatorships.

However, the League is often blamed because it was forced to tolerate the presence and membership and sometimes even the direction of Governments which had no faith in the ideal of international co-operation. These Governments did not understand that the existence of the League had created new duties and new methods.

For seventeen years the League has grown weaker because national egoism has grown stronger. The League duty was to oblige people to think internationally. But, on the contrary, nationalism is still progressing throughout the world, linked with its murderous dogma of national sovereignty.

Yes, the League needs reforming if it is to live, but the basic reform is the one which draws limits to the so-called liberty of action, of independent States, and does away with nationalism. International sovereignty alone can bring about international peace. We are far from it, but democratic France has proved, by the words and by the acts of her statesmen, that she is ready to work through international law for international peace.

CHAPTER XI

SOVIET POLICY AND THE RECONSTRUCTION OF THE LEAGUE

by
ANDREW ROTHSTEIN
Geneva Correspondent for Tass (Soviet News Agency)

BEFORE I proceed to the subject, I should re-state here, I think, what I said last year at the Institute, to avoid any misconceptions: that I am not a Soviet official, and that therefore I am not speaking for the Soviet Government in any sense. I am speaking as a journalist who has worked for the Soviet newspapers for sixteen years, and who therefore has seen something of Soviet foreign policy, and in particular, during the last few years, of the policy of the Soviet delegation in the League of Nations. That is my only claim to the privilege of being allowed to speak to you here.

i. *Why the Soviet Union joined the League.*

The first thing I want to touch on is why the Soviet Union is in the League of Nations at all. The Soviet Government passed very many years of its existence fighting for its life, either by military means or afterwards politically, diplomatically and economically, against the Great Powers who for a number of years dominated the League of Nations. In those years the Soviet Union's opinions of the League of Nations were very sharp and very critical. And yet in 1934, as you know, the Soviet Union entered the League of Nations. Why? Was it that the Soviet Union's approach to the Powers constituting the League of Nations had changed? Was it that it had revised its ideas as to the possibility of co-operating with the capitalist Powers? No. It was because the Great Powers represented in the League of Nations in 1934 were not what they were when they had used the League of Nations in order to dominate the world after the Treaty of Versailles. The circumstances were different. Powers which were down and out in 1918 were preparing for wars of revenge. Other Powers, which had been dissatisfied with the results of the general robbery which took place under the halo of the Versailles Peace Treaty, dissatisfied with their share of the spoils, were preparing for a new division of the world by violence. And the League of Nations, with all its faults and all its weaknesses, was a fetter and a hindrance to them.

On the other hand, there were Powers who for different reasons were interested in the maintenance of peace, some because they stood to lose from any war. They were too small to hope for colonies or other people's territory as the result of a successful war, even if they were on the side of the victors. It would not be they who would benefit. Then there were Powers who were satisfied with the results of the last War, and felt, for one reason or another, that they also would lose by a new war.

For a number of different reasons there were Powers greatly interested in the maintenance of peace, and Powers interested in the promotion of war. And in that situation the League of Nations could no longer play the part of an instrument of the unchallenged hegemony of the

Allied Powers, as it had in 1919 and the years after the War. These were the circumstances in which the Soviet Union decided to enter the League of Nations.

ii. *The Foreign Policy of the Soviet Union.*

For the policy of the Soviet Union in foreign relations, from the first moment of its existence, has been the promotion and preservation of peace. I have not time here to go into the background of all the why and wherefore. I think it sufficient to say that the Soviet Union has abolished the classes interested in taking other people's territory, in exploiting other people's cheap labour, in securing sources of cheap raw materials abroad, or in maintaining a professional military clique whose profession requires aggression. The Soviet Union has fought for peace since 1917, and in 1934 entrance into the League was a practical means of fighting for peace appropriate to the moment.

I could not illustrate that more clearly than in giving you one or two quotations from the pronouncements of people who are better qualified than I am to speak on behalf of the Soviet Union. On December 25, 1933, Stalin gave an interview to Walter Duranty, correspondent of the *New York Times*, in which he said:

'Notwithstanding the withdrawal of Germany and Japan from the League of Nations, or perhaps just because of this, the League may become something of a brake to retard the beginning of military operations, or to hinder them. If this is so, and if the League could prove to be somewhat of an obstruction that could, even to a certain extent, hinder the promotion of war and help in any degree to further the cause of peace, then we are not against the League.'

Three days later the Soviet Prime Minister, Molotov, spoke on foreign policy at a session of the Central Executive Committee of Soviets, saying:

'Even the League of Nations has, to a certain extent, stood in the way of "liberty" for the interventionists' (in China). 'It must be recognized that the League of Nations has exerted a certain restraining influence upon those forces which are preparing for war.'

The third quotation is from the Soviet Government's newspaper, the *Izvestia*, of September 20, 1934, two days after the Soviet Union had entered the League of Nations. It said in an editorial:

'The Soviet Government is entering into the League of Nations in order to support those Powers which will struggle for the preservation and the consolidation of peace.'

I have given these three quotations because I think that they illustrate the purpose, and also the reservations, if you like, with which the Soviet Union entered the League. The Soviet Union did not enter the League because it thought the League was some new panacea, some heaven-sent remedy for settling the affairs of this wicked world. The Soviet Union remained what it was in 1917—the first Socialist Republic: the country where the working-class had for the first time seized power and refashioned society after its own image. The Soviet conception of how the affairs of this world can be settled goes very far beyond such an instrument as the League of Nations. It does not believe, has never believed, that the League of Nations can guarantee final peace, that the League is the only way to preserve peace, or even that it is the chief way to preserve peace. But even with a limited sphere it may act as something of a hindrance in the way of the war-makers.

It may act as an obstacle, an impediment, something that hinders their action. The Soviet Union supports the League, as the Soviet Union has repeatedly supported other things, while not by any means believing that they were what their devoted and sometimes deluded supporters thought them to be—because the League still can play a positive part (be it ever so little) in hindering war.

iii. *The Attitude of the Soviet Union towards the Reform of the League.*

Because of that the Soviet Union is utterly and completely and uncompromisingly against any suggestion of "reform" of the League of Nations! The Soviet Union says that something which may, if its principles are applied 100 per cent, constitute an obstacle or impediment to war, does not require reforming. It does not require tinkering with, interfering with. It requires utilizing to the full.

When, in June 1936, the representative of Chile, which was one of the first States to begin sabotaging sanctions against Italy, moved for reform of the League, and said it was obvious that the Covenant needed reform, Litvinov said he was not at all sure of this. Rather was it necessary to see what could be done to apply the principles and provisions of the Covenant. The next month (July 1936), when the idea was subjected to full-dress debate at the Assembly, Litvinov pointed out that Article 16 of the Covenant—which provides, as you no doubt know, for the application of economic sanctions, and for military sanctions which may be recommended by the Council against the aggressor—enables the League to break any aggressor if it is only applied. And because it

enables the League to break the aggressor, the mere knowledge that there are sufficient Powers ready to apply
sanctions will be enough in nine cases out of ten to deter
the aggressor. But if the aggressor nevertheless pursues
his policy in different parts of the world, the policy of
actually preparing or carrying on aggression, it is because
he has not that certainty that there are a sufficient
nnmber of Powers ready to apply Article 16.

Litvinov said:

> 'I am far from idealizing the Covenant. Its imperfections
> consist, not so much in its articles, as in its omissions and
> obscurities. Therefore one has to speak, not of reforming the
> Covenant, but of making it more precise and of reinforcing it.'

And he went on to indicate what, in the opinion of the
Soviet Government, are these imperfections.

First of all, there is no definition of aggression. You may
remember it was the Soviet Government at the Disarmament Conference which initiated the discussion of a definition of aggression, and which actually got that definition
adopted by a Conference Committee. There the definition would have remained, buried in the files, but that the
Soviet Government in 1933 got thirteen States to sign a
convention recognizing this definition. Had this definition
of aggression been adopted by the countries constituting
the League today, there would have been no doubt about
all members of the League having to apply sanctions
against Italy during her war on Ethiopia, the Japanese
would not have been able to do what they are doing in
Manchuria and China today, etc., let alone what both
Germany and Italy are doing in Spain. All these cases
of the modern 'war which is not war' are provided for
explicitly in this definition of aggression.

Litvinov pointed out, furthermore, that there was no clarity as to who registers the fact of aggression. There was no clarity as to the binding character of sanctions; and we saw during the Italian war on Abyssinia that there were countries which justified their failure to apply sanctions by appealing to national sovereignty, and to rights which everybody thought they had renounced by signing the international treaty constituting the Covenant of the League of Nations. People sometimes forget that the Covenant is not just what its name is often interpreted to mean, a kind of solemn pledge in general terms, but is an international treaty of the same character as any other international treaty. Yet because of lack of clarity as to the binding character of its obligations, many a Government was able to refuse to fulfil its obligations under the Covenant, as during the aggression against Abyssinia.

The Covenant again lacks clarity as to when sanctions are to be applied. In any case, he said, why should the Covenant be reformed? For whose sake? The argument was used openly by some, covertly by others, that it was necessary to reform the Covenant because otherwise we could not have universality. Here was Litvinov's reply, which I will permit myself to quote because it puts the matter in a nutshell:

'To whose state of mind, then, should the Covenant be adapted? Of those who take their stand on the consistent and collective defence of security, who see the highest interest of all nations in the maintenance of universal peace, who consider that in the long run this is required by the interests of every State, that this can be achieved only by sacrificing temporary interests to the community of nations, and who are ready even to place part of their own armed forces at the disposal of that community? Or of those who, in principle, swear allegiance to the principle of collective security, but in practice are prepared to apply it only when it coincides with the interests of their own country. Or of those who on principle reject collective security, replace international solidarity with the watchword "Sauve qui peut," preach the localization of war and proclaim war itself to be the highest manifestation of the human spirit? I fear that it is precisely the last category of persons whom people have in mind when they argue the necessity of adapting—or, as I would call it, degrading—the Covenant, since they reinforce their argument by asserting that in this way States which have left the League may be brought back. Thus we are asked at all costs to restore to the League States which left it only because they see obstacles to the fulfilment of their aggressive intentions in the Covenant, in Articles 10 and 16, in sanctions. We are told, "Throw Article 10 out of the Covenant, throw out Article 16, renounce sanctions, reject collective security, and then former members of the League may return to our ranks, and the League become universal." In other words, " Let us make the League safe for aggressors." I say that we don't need a League which is safe for aggressors with all its universality, since such a League, from an instrument of peace, will turn into its very opposite. At best, by depriving the League of the functions of collective security, we should be turning it into a debating society or a charitable institution unworthy of the name of League of Nations, unworthy of the resources spent on it and not answering to those hopes and anticipations which are grounded upon it.'

When the next month, in August 1936, in reply to a circular inquiry from the Secretariat, the Soviet Union sent its proposals for reinforcing the Covenant, or for better application of the principles of the Covenant, the Soviet Government again reiterated, 'The revision of the Covenant of the League of Nations cannot be regarded as justified by circumstances.' When there was the big debate in the Assembly on this question in September 1936, Litvinov repeated this frontal attack on those who believed that you should modify the League, modify the Covenant, or reconstruct the League in order to make it more palatable for the aggressor.   He said:

'I would object even more strongly if, in the name of universality, the League were to set about eliminating from the Covenant all that makes it a weapon of peace and a threat to the aggressor.   I should object vigorously to anything calculated, as I said at the last session of the Assembly, to make the League safe for the aggressor.   Of course, a State which openly exalts the power of the sword as against international obligations, for which it does not conceal its contempt: a power which cynically calls on other States to adopt the same contemptuous attitude to their signature at the foot of treaties, with the object of finally destroying international confidence : such a power cannot feel comfortable in a League of Nations which proclaims one of its principal aims to be "the maintenance of justice and the scrupulous respect for all treaty obligations in the dealing of organized peoples with one another."

'A State which is governed by men who have incorporated into the programme of their foreign policy the conquest of other nations' territory, who at their festivities, before their people and the representatives of other States, enumerate the vast territories which they intend violently to separate from other countries, cannot sincerely accept Article 10, which ensures to all member States their territorial integrity and political independence.   A State which preaches the legality of so-called "localized" wars cannot make its peace with Article 16, which proclaims that resort to war against one member of the League is deemed to be an act of war against all other members of the League, and which prescribes a graduated system of sanctions against the aggressor.   Again, here in Geneva, under the auspices of the League of Nations, a convention was signed the other day which prohibits even the mere incitement by wireless to breaches of internal peace in other States.   Can a State sincerely accede to the principles of such a convention which, as has been abundantly proved, maintains in all countries its agencies and secret services, built up of its own nationals, which actively interfere in the life of those

countries, incite party against party, organize and finance insur-
rections, and openly afford military aid to rebels ? Can we
declare compatible with the principle of equality of nations, which
is one of the foundation-stones of the League, the ideology of a
State founded on racial and national inequality, and describing
all peoples except its own as "subhuman"?

'I would ask the supporters of "universality at any price":
must we sacrifice all the fundamental principles of the League
in order to adapt it to the theory and practice of such a State, or
must we invite the latter itself to adapt its principles to the
present ideology of the League? My reply, at any rate, is:
Better a League without universality than universality without
League principles.'

iv. *The Soviet Union's Proposals for Strengthening the Covenant.*

And now we come to the actual Soviet proposals for
reinforcing the League. At the outset I told you what,
in the mind of the people of the Soviet Union, is the state
of the world today. On the one hand we have the bloc
of the aggressors. It is a united bloc—some of them united
by what they call an 'axis,' others united for what they
call defence against the Communist International. You
only have to watch the newspapers to see how perfectly
their actions are co-ordinated. Their aggression is quite
open, quite unashamed.

Last year, I remember, at this Institute there were still
some people not entirely convinced by the quotations I
gave from *Mein Kampf* about the principles of aggression
which underlie the political doctrine of the Third Reich,
and who maintained that I had not given sufficient weight
to all the declarations Hitler had been making about his
anxiety for peace. He had wanted agreement with France

and agreement with England: he was ready to negotiate non-aggression pacts. All of these things, I pointed out, did not stand in the way of aggression at all, because they all fitted perfectly into the famous scheme under which Germany would become a kind of 'one-way gun' for one-way aggression—aggression that would go off to her east, not to her west.

But I think that even those people today, after the events of the last twelve months, after what we have seen happening in Spain and in China, would not hesitate to admit that there is a clear and well-defined bloc of aggressors in the world, and all their peaceful declarations are not worth the paper on which they are written.

What do we see on the other hand? The Powers interested in the maintenance of peace for a variety of reasons (even for selfish reasons), together with the great majority of people in all countries, including the aggressor countries, represent a great majority in favour of peace. But that majority is not co-ordinated, is not organized. There is no peace front, no centre of co-operation for resisting the aggressor, for deterring the aggressor, which would incidentally act as a moral support for those immense forces of opposition to the aggressor in his own country.

The Soviet delegation here at the League again and again has stressed the disastrous nature of such a situation. Here is what Litvinov said in the same Assembly speech in September 1936:

'I have not the slightest doubt that even the most politically inexperienced reader of the newspapers knows which and how many are the countries whose aggressiveness makes them dangerous, if they are only familiar with the speeches and writings of the rulers of these countries. There are also some countries which strive to seek salvation in neutrality. If they really believe that it would be sufficient for them to write the word "neutrality" on their frontiers, there to arrest the flames of war, and if they have forgotten the recent lessons of history as to breaches of even internationally recognized neutralities, that is their affair. We have the right, at least, to ask them already to observe their neutrality today, when some are preparing plans of aggression and others plans for self-defence. Unfortunately, they are often already placing their neutrality at the service of the forces of aggression. By the side of these professedly neutral countries there are a number of others, including some of the most powerful States in the world, who undoubtedly see the storm-cloud advancing over Europe, understand its threatening character, feel the peril inevitably involved for themselves and, it would seem, recognize the necessity of common defence, declaring again and again their adherence to the principle of collective security. We regret to see that, so far, they do not go beyond these declarations, and are doing nothing to clothe the idea of collective security in a suitable form, or to give it effective power, in the vain hope that the aggressor, taking heed of their exhortations, will undergo a change of heart and help them to restrain his aggression. But the aggressor, who is basing all his policy on superiority in brute material force, with only threatening demands, bluff, menaces and the tactics of *faits accomplis* in the arsenal of his diplomacy, is accessible only to the voice of a policy no less firm than his own, and to a cold calculation of the relative strength of forces. Any exhortations and entreaties, and still more concessions to his illegal and senseless demands, any economic bribes offered to him, merely produce in him an impression of weakness, confirm his consciousness of his own power, and encourage him to further intransigence and illegalities. Even outside his frontiers the legend of his invincibility may arise, and thus give birth to a fatalist and pusillanimous mood in certain countries, which gradually—sometimes even without noticing it—may lose their independence and become the vassals of the aggressor. In this way begins the process of creating a hegemony, to be completed by the military subjugation of the countries which refuse to submit voluntarily.

G*

'Yes, ladies and gentlemen, we must not close our eyes to the existence of aspirations for hegemony, for the hegemony of of a "chosen people," called by history itself, so it is alleged, to dominate all other peoples, whom it pronounces to be of an inferior class. I will refer in passing to the ideological consequences of such a hegemony, and to the violent destruction of all the treasures of mind and culture which were the pride of humanity in recent centuries, and the artificial resurrection of ideas belonging to the worst period of the Middle Ages. Yet the aggregate power of the peace-loving countries, both in the economic and in the military sense, their total resources in man-power and in the war industries, considerably surpass the strength of any possible combination of countries which the aggressor might rally around him. I am deeply convinced that it would be sufficient for these forces in some way to combine, to display merely the possibility of joint action, for the peril of war to be averted, and for the aggressor to be obliged to ask, sooner or later, to be admitted himself to the common system of collective security.'

All the Soviet proposals for reinforcing the League, for strengthening application of the Covenant, are based on this conviction that this is the situation we see in the world today, and that it is necessary to create a centre of resistance to aggression—without believing that it is the final guarantee against war. There is no final guarantee against war until the causes for war have been eliminated—the struggle for markets, exploitation of man by man. To that belief the Soviet Union holds as strongly as it did in 1917.

But, short of that, the League remains a very powerful means of hindering war. What, then, were the proposals which the Soviet Government made for reinforcement of the League?

They fall into two main classes. The first class of proposals is to improve the procedure of the League, in order to make it more effective. The second class of proposals is, in the words of the Soviet reply to the League, 'proposals to constitute a supplementary guarantee of security within the framework of the Covenant' by 'mutual assistance agreements between States concerned in the maintenance of security in specific areas.'

Now what are the first series of proposals? They are mainly directed to prevent what I am sure must have seemed to all of you, again and again, at critical moments, an intolerable delay and procrastination with which situations are dealt with, and in which we know that thousands of men and women and children are being massacred. That is not overstating the case. And so the Soviet Government proposed that a special resolution might be adopted, which should provide that, within three days after war had been begun and a complaint submitted to the League by any Power, the Council should meet within three days, and that within another three days it should give a decision. That decision, instead of requiring unanimity, shall be considered adopted when there is a three-fourths majority, whether it is to declare there is a war of aggression taking place, or to say there is no war, in which case all the provisions about sanctions would not come into play. Within six days after an appeal has been made, every Member of the League is *ipso facto* considered at war with the aggressor: 'the enemy of one is the enemy of all.' Economic sanctions adopted in this way by a three-fourths majority are binding on every Member of the League. We shall not then have the tragic and humiliating spectacle which we saw when sanctions were decided on against Italy, and when some Powers actually remained in the League and talked nonsense about loyalty to League principles, and yet did not raise one finger to share the common sacrifice—on the contrary, secretly assisted the aggressor. So, the Soviet proposals suggest that failure to take part in sanctions would involve trade and customs restrictions against these Powers. This was proposed by the Soviet Government during the Italo-Ethiopian dispute, and was shelved, like other Soviet proposals. Then the Soviet Union proposed that there should be no loopholes for long delay on the pretext of putting these sanctions into law. The Soviet Government proposed that every State Member of the League of Nations must pass the necessary legislation, in accordance with the constitution of its own country, so as to make sanctions immediately possible when they were called for. In other words, home legislation should be brought in line with international obligations.

Lastly, in order to facilitate the work of the Council, the League should adopt a just definition of the aggressor, so that to send armies or aeroplanes across another country's frontier, or to take other war steps, would be just as much an act of aggression as similar acts if carried out after a formal declaration of war. None of the usual excuses of protection of life and property, dangerous social disturbances, etc., could be used as excuses for sending troops over other people's frontiers, aeroplanes over other people's frontiers, ships into other people's ports. You will realize, by the way, that in opposition to this the Soviet Government found ranged against it not only the Powers outside the League, but also Powers which were inside the League, and were at least as interested in excuses of this kind as Powers outside which had perhaps not as many battleships.

v. *The Need for Pacts of Mutual Assistance.*

Secondly came the proposals to supplement the League Covenant by mutual assistance agreements. Why are these necessary? This is essential, I think, for us all to be clear upon, for there has been more confusion, and dangerous confusion, about this than about any other issue. First and fundamental: an aggressor in the world today can be restrained only by force. So far as the Soviet Union is concerned, you will understand that the workers and peasants did not come into power by Tolstoyan methods, and consequently they have no intention of adopting Tolstoyan methods in dealing with their enemies at home or abroad. Experience of the world, of the League of Nations itself, has justified the principle that force has to be met with force. You cannot deal with Hitler and Mussolini by turning the other cheek or by offering them a hymn-book. The Covenant of the League is based on that principle. It says so in Articles 8 and 16.

Next, unfortunately, owing to the diversity of their interests, the different Powers constituting the League are at present unable all to take part at one time in the force restraining an aggressor. The Soviet Union has its explanation of that. You do not expect me here to give you a statement of Marxist and Leninist principles, but I think you do not have to be a Marxist, or even to know that it is the nature of the capitalist system which is responsible, to see when you look at the world today that different Powers have such a diversity of interests. It is sometimes doubtful whether they will even strike a blow in their own defence. But they certainly won't strike a blow against an aggressor in some distant part of the world—distant, I mean, from their own immediate interests.

Therefore, we are forced back upon some less universal means of applying this force, and of threatening to apply it when the aggressor is threatening aggression. On the other hand, if we abandon the victim completely to the aggressor, as Litvinov has said, the result is only to encourage the aggressor. Do we need any proof of that after these last two years? Take Japan's policy. It is now six years since here, in Geneva, a representative of China published the full Tanaka memorandum, drawn up by a Prime Minister of Japan, in which stage by stage plans for the annexation of China and Asia were set out. And step by step, during the last six years, you will find that that memorandum has been applied. And why has it been applied? Because in 1931, when the first step in its application was taken by the invasion and annexation of Manchuria, the League capitulated, and the Great Powers, who were under obligation to each other to protect China, surrendered. During the last two years we have seen in succeeding steps the same process with Italy. In the war of aggression against Abyssinia, we know that at the crucial moment oil sanctions were rejected, because there was fear that this might lead to force. The Powers were actually afraid of having to apply a little force, in other words, of becoming involved in war with Italy. The net result of the unpunished war against Abyssinia has been the far less punished war of aggression against Spain.

So force is required to restrain the aggressor. But the Powers will not all take part in applying that force at one time. On the other hand, to abandon the victim means to encourage the aggressor. What other conclusions are possible but that the Powers interested should join together to carry out their obligations under the Covenant, come what may? In other words, undertake as a duty what the Covenant gives them permission to do. Soviet experience shows that working for such local pacts is working to keep the peace. The proposals for a mutual assistance pact with Poland and Germany to guarantee the independence of the Baltic States in 1934, three or four months later the proposals for an Eastern Locarno, and, lastly, the proposal for a three-power pact of France, U.S.S.R. and Germany to guarantee one another's European frontiers, all served this purpose. Germany successively rejected these three pacts, which was more eloquent evidence of what the foreign policy of the German Reich was based on than any propaganda declaration or speech would have been.

vi. *The Character of these Pacts.*

What is the character of these mutual assistance pacts by which the Soviet Union proposes to clear up the obscurities in the Covenant of the League? First of all, they only come into force when a signatory is the victim of aggression. And all the Powers in the regions concerned have the right of joining the pacts, with all the privileges and obligations ensuing therefrom. There can be no exclusion. It is not a case of simple alliance against a third power, as in the old pre-War alliances. The pacts come into force only when aggression has taken place.

On this point I will read you one more remark by Litvinov which he made when the Council met in London on March 17th 1936, after German troops marched into the Rhineland. He was then speaking on non-aggression pacts, but the principle is the same. He said:

'The Soviet Union has itself signed pacts of non-aggression with its neighbours (excepting Japan, which rejects such a pact to this day). But the Soviet Union has always attached great importance to the point that *these pacts should not facilitate aggression against third parties.*

'We, therefore, always included in these pacts a special clause, freeing either of the contracting parties from any obligations under the pact if the other party commits an act of aggression against a third State. Such a clause, however, will be absent from the pacts proposed by Mr. Hitler, according to the model which he has indicated.

'And, without such a clause, the proposed system of pacts reduces itself to the principle of localization of war which is preached by Mr. Hitler. Every State which has signed such a pact with Germany is immobilized by her in the event of Germany attacking a third State.'

Next, the pacts come into play only in circumstances in which the Covenant itself recognizes the right of assistance. Two kinds of circumstance justifying mutual assistance are recognized by the Covenant: first, when the Council of the League has declared that a state of aggression exists, and second, when it has failed to come to an agreement, in which case Members of the League are authorized to take such action which they feel is 'necessary for the maintenance of right and justice.' These two cases, in which the forces of the pacts proposed by the Soviet Union would come into effect, are entirely within the framework of the League, and this has been recognized by Britain, France and other States.

Thirdly, these mutual assistance pacts must be registered

and published, like all the other treaties since Article 18 of the Covenant was adopted, laying it down that treaties not registered at Geneva would not be binding. As a matter of fact, there are already in existence treaties in which members of the League take part which are in defiance of this proposal. The Soviet Union proposes this safeguard. Finally, once war has been notified, the countries concerned have the right to take all necessary steps to prepare their armed forces to give assistance. They cannot actually take warlike action, but they can begin their preparations.

There have been one or two objections raised to these pacts. One objection, voiced here last year by my good friend and colleague, Clarence Streit, was a technical military objection. He said: Supposing you have a three-power regional pact, of say, France, Germany and Great Britain. It is to provide for joint action against an aggressor in case any of the three breaks the peace. What happens? England has to have a military agreement with Germany against France, and with France against Germany: Germany an agreement with Britain against France, and with France against Britain: and so on. He said that, technically, difficulties would arise which would make the operation of the pacts impossible, because States would have to reveal their military secrets to each other.

With all due respect, I think that is not a true difficulty at all. It is possible to postpone actual plans for military support and yet to deter the aggressor. Surely the prospect of military support after aggression has begun is better than no military support at all, as it is at present.

Take an example. Suppose (for the sake of argument) that there is a country in the world which is undergoing military aggression on the part of a group of armed law-breakers. The victim of aggression is exceptionally weak in military equipment. A number of countries are under obligation to that attacked country to come to its assistance. Most countries have broken that obligation. Only one country has come to the assistance of the attacked State. The assistance began only after aggression had started. Can anyone say, however, that such assistance might not, at a crucial moment, be of 100 per cent importance to the country attacked? Could you not conceive of the statesmen of that country declaring: 'If it were not for that assistance, we should not be in existence today?'

Secondly, it has been a commonplace for years that every Great Power has pigeonholed in its War Office plans for war of the very kind spoken of in 1936—plans for war with A against B, with B against A, with A and B against C, etc. There is not the final link, but not far short of it.

A more serious objection is that of the creation of 'ideological' blocs. You can see what seems to be an 'ideological' bloc between German Nazism and Italian Fascism. I am not quite sure about the exact 'ideological' bloc which connects the Aryans of the Third Reich with the Samurai of Japan. I am not sure whether ideology would stand up against material interests if Germany and Italy had differences about the latter. But where would be the 'ideological' bloc between countries like the French Republic, the British Empire, the Union of Soviet Socialist Republics? With totally different social and political systems in the Soviet Union and the capitalist States, where would be the ideological bloc, if all of them got together and said: 'No more aggression'?

I think I can clinch this point with another observation by Litvinov, at the 1936 Assembly:

'Are you calling for the formation of blocs, someone may ask me. I know that for some super-pacifists the word "bloc" has become a bugbear. No, I am not asking for new blocs. I am quite satisfied with a bloc which exists already, and which bears the name of the League of Nations, a bloc of countries that want peace and that have united for that purpose of mutual defence and mutual aid. All we ask is that this bloc should genuinely organize mutual aid: that it should draw up its plan of action well ahead, so as not to be taken by surprise: and that the organization of war which is taking place outside this bloc should be answered by effective action for the organization of collective resistance. It may be that not all the countries at present constituting the bloc known as the League of Nations wish to participate in such action. It may be that there are some among them who think security is to be found in the word "neutrality," or who hope at the last minute to desert to the side of the aggressor. But this in no way deprives of the right of joint action those who can and wish to defend themselves, and who have no desire to be attacked one by one.'

I hope that now I have brought out what I was driving at—the essential underlying principle of which is that the Soviet Union does not want to 'reform' the League. I think reform of the League is a device of those Powers who wish to break up the League. The Soviet Union wants to strengthen the League as an instrument for helping to maintain peace in the world.

CHAPTER XII

CURRENT CRITICISMS OF THE PEACE FRONT

by

Sir NORMAN ANGELL

IN a previous paper I suggested that the underlying principles of the League could still be made a reality in international politics if Britain were to take the lead in the formation of a Peace Bloc, or an international 'Peace Front.' The Peace Bloc could grow from the present alliance of Britain and France enlarged by the firmer adhesion of Russia, those States forming the nucleus of a group whose defence would be organized on a collective basis, on the principle, that is, that an attack on one was an attack on all. Mutual defence should, however, only constitute one side of the policy which they supported in common. They should, in effect, say to the totalitarian States:

'While we shall all resist attack upon any one of us, we do not stand for the unchangeability of the *status quo*. We are prepared to afford the fullest opportunities for investigation of grievances or disabilities; to go fully into such questions as access to raw materials; to establish in the non-self-governing colonies a system ensuring real equality of economic opportunity; to create institutions of peaceful change. Thus, while the road of conquest and violence as a means of remedying your economic difficulties is blocked by our power, the road of peaceful change is opened. We are prepared ourselves to abide by the principles of third-party judgment we ask you to observe. We are prepared to fight, not that we may impose our one-sided judgment upon you, but to prevent you imposing your one-sided judgment upon us; not to prevent changes in the *status quo*, but to prevent changes by your violence to our disadvantage; not to close empires against you, but to see that you do not by conquest close them against us. And we ask you to join us in maintaining these principles and avail yourselves of the law against violence which we are prepared to defend in common.'

i. *Is it Fair to Germany?*

One of the commonest objections against such a policy is that it constitutes 'coercion' of totalitarian States, their 'encirclement,' and that it will precipitate the 'war of ideologies.'

Let us be clear, first, as to what we mean by 'coercion' and 'encirclement,' and whether the proposal I have made is in any sense more 'coercive' or 'encircling' than that programme of immense national rearmament plus alliance with France which those who criticize the Peace Bloc usually support.

If Britain were the victim of unprovoked aggression on the part of some continental power, and fought to defend its soil, is it guilty of 'coercing' the enemy?

If, realizing that we by our own forces are so inferior to a potential enemy as to be undefended, we arrange with France for mutual assistance in resisting him, and he attacks, is *that* coercion?

If to two nations thus combined for common defence are added others—say a group of small States like Belgium—does this addition make a 'coercive League' so severely condemned by these critics?

They must be aware that we must make an alliance or

abandon defence altogether. The only way to deprive such an alliance of danger is to make it clear that it does not stand for the 'encirclement' of those outside it, because it is open to them to join it; to make it clear that the members are ready to offer to others the same means of defence they claim for themselves; the same rights, in return for the same obligations.

Alliances we are going to have. If they stand for the defence not of this or that State, but of a principle of defence which creates equality of right, if, that is, they are to lose the very element of danger which made them disastrous before 1914, then, and only then it would seem, do they become the thing these critics condemn.

A recent letter to the *Times*, signed in common by complete pacifists and by ardent advocates of a great rearmament programme, contains the following passage:

> 'To commit ourselves not only to economic but to automatic military action, instead of *equipping the League to do justice as between nations, is simply to increase and diminish the risk of explosion.* It will inevitably result in dividing the world into two great military alliances, the one standing for the *status quo*, the other for the revision of it.'

The signatories of the letter suggest that the League will be better equipped to 'do justice between nations'—modify frontiers, attentuate economic nationalism, reduce armaments, ensure equality of right—if it does not concern itself with the problem of defence (the defence, that is, of its constituent members), although it is quite obvious that the main motive of the unjust frontiers, the struggle for economic self-sufficiency, great armaments, is national security, the determination of every State to ensure, first of all, its safety. Guns before butter. 'Self-preservation is the first law.'

Note the real meaning of this demand that the League, while making no provision at all for the satisfaction of the deepest of all national impulses (which is indeed the deepest impulse of all living things), shall nevertheless modify frontiers which are unsound, abate economic nationalism, limit armaments, give to Germany the equality which is her natural right. A State, already fearful for its security, is asked by its neighbours to weaken itself by revision of some frontier at present strategically advantageous, by surrender of territory, by lessening its economic self-sufficiency, reducing its armaments. But it is told at the same time that it must expect no help from those who make these demands if it is attacked as the result of complying with them.

That is not realism; it is not equity. Remedy of grievances, 'revision,' is not an alternative to the policy of collective security. The latter is the condition *sine qua non* of being able to carry any just revision into effect; of any hope of change in the *status quo* except by war, which means change at the dictation of the victor, the last status in that case being worse than the first. To argue 'there can be no security till we get justice' is to invert the truth, which is that we shall never get justice till we have managed to organize our common defence on a mutual and collective basis.

The only solution for Germany's economic difficulties, for instance, is an international one. But Germany rejects economic internationalism because, for purposes of defence, she desires to be economically self-sufficient. She will not abandon that effort unless her security (from, say, Russia or France) is assured. If that security is to rest upon Germany's preponderance, then her neighbours are insecure, as the war proved. Only by the collective method can the security of one be made compatible with that of the other; or economic internationalism, indispensable to welfare, reconciled with defence.

When, many years ago, this particular 'pro-German' urged that we give unequivocally to France the guarantees of defence which we have given only recently, the proposal was usually criticized as an attempt to 'encircle' Germany. It was, in fact, the only means by which better treatment of Germany could have been obtained. France said in effect to Britain: 'If you do not give us adequate guarantees of defence against renewal of German invasion, we must take our own methods to weaken Germany.' Thus the Ruhr invasion, wildly applauded ('Hats off to France') by the very Press which now criticizes the advocates of collective security for 'making trouble with Germany.' The real purpose of giving the guarantees to France was to ensure that, with her fears about security removed, she would behave well to Germany. The guarantees, so perversely represented as 'coercion' of Germany, were designed to prevent, and, if given, would have prevented, coercions like those of the Ruhr invasion. The situation illustrates the truth that there can be no just revision or effective peaceful change unless nations feel safe. For otherwise they will retain unjust frontiers, develop economic self-sufficiency, continue in all the other mischief that keeps Europe in a turmoil. Again, redress of grievances is not the alternative to collective security: it is the condition of any effective redress of grievances whatever.

ii. *Will it turn Local Wars into World Wars?*

The signatories of the letter I have quoted from—some of whom are ardent advocates of rearmament—imply that defence must be organized unilaterally, each his own defender, as in the years that led to 1914. The collective method, they say, will turn every local war into a world war. Yet when a shot in a Balkan village—a 'local' war indeed—actually did involve practically the whole world, the result was not due to the entanglements of the League or the collective system, for those things did not exist. Nor did Britain and Germany drift to war because of unresolved specific differences between them, because, that is, Germany was making demands (as today she is demanding territory) which we felt we had to refuse, or vice versa. The War arose out of the fears which each entertained of the growing power of the other, out of that system of each defending himself or his interests and not any agreed rule of peace, the system which the signatories imply is preferable to any alternative collective method.

At the time of the Abyssinian crisis I ventured to suggest that if we really meant what our Government is always saying about the Covenant being the 'keystone,' the 'sheet anchor,' the 'life-line' of our foreign policy; if, indeed, we had regarded the defence of the Covenant to be as important as the defence, say, of some small West Indian island, this crisis would never have arisen and the peace of the world would have been preserved.

Italy knows that an attempt to seize, say, Malta would be resisted by all the power of the British Empire. Therefore its seizure is not attempted. The British policy of so defending British territory does not involve war. Nor would a similar definiteness of intention to defend the Covenant, had that intention been sufficiently plain in time, have involved war. It is uncertainty as to what we would do that in truth explains the drift to war. While Italy knows that there would be no question at all about our defending Australia or New Zealand, or for that matter St. Kitts in the West Indies, defending them single-handed, without talking of the difficulties into which we might get with the United States on account of blockade or what not, Italy also knows, unhappily, that we are in two minds about the defence of the Covenant. And upon that uncertainty, that division of will, the military dictator is ready to gamble.

Our difficulty, therefore, is not in the last analysis a material one, a lack of means and power, but absence of any clear conviction as to how that power may best be used defensively. On behalf of the tiniest British colony seized by a foreign State the whole power of the Empire would be invoked, not because of the intrinsic importance of that particular morsel of territory, but because to yield thus the defensive principle in one instance would sooner or later lead to its impotence everywhere.

We get this absurdity: Defence without war for the tiniest and remotest colony can be secured by Britain's sole power, acting 'silently.' Defence for a principle upon which rests the whole of civilization (including presumably the Empire) cannot be secured at all.

Something over a hundred years ago, at the suggestion of a British statesman, the then weak and feeble United States proclaimed the doctrine that any attempt to conquer an American State would be regarded as an attack upon itself. By so doing the United States established a collective system of defence for the Western Hemisphere as against European 'expansion.' The United States did not wait for the agreement of the twenty nations of the American continent. It gave a lead which, within the intended limits, has been successful. A similar lead on this side of the world by a State far more powerful than was then the United States would give an equally successful result.

iii. *A Policy for Pacifists.*

If Germany—or Italy—accepts the offer of that Peace Bloc I have described, she will in fact have accepted the League of Nations. Meantime we should in any case combine our power with those who do in fact accept these League principles. But let us be careful to go on proclaiming for the world to hear that such a policy does not involve the encirclement of Germany or Italy; that there is a standing invitation for them to come in; that such a combination claims for itself no principle of security it does not willingly accord to others; membership would defend Germany as much as any other nation belonging to the combination. That is not encirclement, and it would be the road to peace.

It is not the policy which we have been following. We have not been applying the collective system because large sections of our people simply do not believe in it.

If we had made the most of the American offer to co-operate with us in resisting Japan in 1931—an offer which we refused—it is extremely unlikely that Mussolini would have attacked Abyssinia; and if that had been prevented he would not have intervened in Spain. The failure of legal force in the restraint of Italy has not meant less force and brutality in the world. It has meant more force, more ferocity, more cynicism and evil; and less peace.

When militarists come to Pacifists and say, 'Let us keep and increase our armament to be used in the good old way each for himself, announcing clearly that our armaments will never be used for League purposes because we are agreed that the League should not rest on force '—if such a proposal is carried, as it is sometimes carried, with the help of Pacifists, it means a victory, not for the Pacifist element in international affairs but the militarist element. To say, 'Let us remove force from the law but keep it for the litigants is not to reduce but to increase the chances of force being used, to make conflict indeed inevitable.

Pacifists should be sure which question they are answering. If the question is, 'Should force be used,' the Pacifist, given his convictions, can answer without hesitation, 'No.' But suppose the question is something entirely different, namely, 'The force being there, is it better to use it under a constitution upholding equal rights, or to let each party to a dispute use it to enforce his own judgment on a rival?' If that is the question, there is only one reply the Pacifist can give, namely, that bad as force may be, it is better as the instrument of a constitution than as a means whereby each party attempts to enforce his judgment on the other.

There are some of us who do not believe in capital punishment. But we support courts enforcing it because the alternative—anarchy and chaos—would be even worse than the present death-inflicting courts. We support the courts, not because we approve capital punishment, but because we do not approve anarchy, which would mean the infliction of more death sentences than ever.

However sceptical we may be of making the possession

of arms compatible with peace, it is our duty, so long as the arms are there, to see that they become the instruments of the better instead of the worse policy.

A convinced Pacifist confronted with the choice of voting for, say, Mr. Lansbury or Sir Oswald Mosley, would vote for Mr. Lansbury; it is conceivable that if he had to choose between Mr. Lansbury and Mr. Dalton or Lord Cecil, the Pacifist would choose Mr. Lansbury. But if the choice is between a Dalton-Cecil policy and a Mosley policy, can a Pacifist refuse to support Dalton and Cecil on the ground that they stand for the employment of force in the last resort? If the result is to give power into the hands of the extreme militarists, and to defeat the Daltons and the Cecils, has the Pacifist promoted his ideals or rendered them immensely more difficult of accomplishment?

Let us not make the best the enemy of the better.

APPENDIX

CONTENTS OF PROBLEMS OF PEACE
(Eleventh Series)

CONTENTS OF PROBLEMS OF PEACE

(Tenth Series)

CHAPTER VI

Peace in the Far East and the Collective System. By Dr. Guy H. Scholefield, O.B.E., Librarian, General Assembly Library, Wellington, New Zealand; Member of the Institute of Pacific Relations.

CHAPTER VII

The Social Basis of World Order. By R. J. P. Mortished, of the International Labour Office.

CHAPTER VIII

International Administration. By E. J. Phelan, Assistant Director of the International Labour Office.

H*

CONTENTS OF PROBLEMS OF PEACE
(Ninth Series)

Introduction.

CHAPTER XI

_____

CONTENTS OF PROBLEMS OF PEACE

(Eighth Series)

CHAPTER I

CHAPTER II

Nationalism and the League of Nations Today.   By Professor William E. Rappard, Director of the Graduate Institute of International Studies, Geneva.

  i. Introduction
  ii. The Sino-Japanese Conflict
  iii. Disarmament
  iv. The Economic Conference
  v. Conclusions.

CHAPTER III

Disarmament and Security.   By W. Arnold-Forster, author of *The Disarmament Conference*, etc.

  i. The Objectives
  ii. Disarmament History
  iii The British Draft Convention
      (*a*) Security
      (*b*) Effectives
      (*c*) Land Material
      (*d*) Naval Material
      (*e*) Air Material
      (*f*) Chemical War
      (*g*) Permanent Disarmament Commission
      (*h*) Termination of the Convention
      (*i*) Expenditure
      (*j*) Arms Traffic and Manufacture
  iv. A Policy.

CHAPTER IV

The Manufacture of Arms and the Arms Traffic.   By Henri Rolin, Legal Adviser to the Belgian Ministry of Foreign Affairs.

  i. The Fundamental Importance of Control
  ii. Article 8 of the Covenant of the League
  iii. Moral and Political Objections to Private Manufacture
  iv. The Temporary Mixed Commission
  v. The Convention of 1925
  vi. The Work of the Council: Draft Convention of 1929

CHAPTER V

Public Opinion and the League of Nations. By E. J. Phelan, Chief of the Diplomatic Division of the International Labour Office.

CHAPTER VI

Recent Territorial Disputes before the League of Nations. By Manley O. Hudson, Bemis Professor International Law, Harvard University.

CHAPTER VII

The Far East Dispute from the Point of View of the Small States. By Sean Lester, Permanent Delegate of the Irish Free State, Geneva.

CHAPTER XI

The World Monetary and Economic Conference. By Clarence K Streit, Geneva Correspondent for the *New York Times*

CHAPTER XII

Public Works and the World Crisis. By P. W. Martin, Research Division of the International Labour Office.

CHAPTER XIII

Recent American Legislation and its Effects on International Relations. By A. H. Feller, Instructor in the Law School, Harvard University.

CONTENTS OF PROBLEMS OF PEACE

(Seventh Series)

CHAPTER II

The World Economic Crisis: Its Causes and Cure. By Sir George Paish, formerly Adviser to the Chancellor of the Exchequer and to the British Treasury on Financial and Economic Questions.

CHAPTER III

The League in Relation to the World Crisis. By William E. Rappard, Director of the Graduate Institute of International Studies, Geneva.

CHAPTER IV

The Results of the Lausanne Conference. By Dr. J. van Walre de Bordes, Member of the Financial Section of the Secretariat of the League of Nations.

v. The 'Treasury Mind'
vi. The New Problem: 'Consumption'
vii. Changing Populations
viii. Competition for Markets
xi. A Plan to Meet the Common Needs of Ordinary Men.

APPENDIX

Conference for the Reduction and Limitation of Armaments: Text of the Resolution adopted by the General Commission on 22 July, 1932.

CONTENTS OF PROBLEMS OF PEACE
(Sixth Series)

CHAPTER I

The League as a Confederation. By Robert Redslob, Professor of International Law in the University of Strasburg.

i. Some Earlier Confederations
ii. Is the League a Confederation?
   (*a*) The Psychological Argument
   (*b*) The Constitution of the League
   (*c*) Its Aims
   (*d*) Its Organs
   (*e*) Reasons for Classing the League as a Confederation
   (*f*) Some Differences.
iii. Conclusion.

CHAPTER II

Public Opinion and the World Community. By Paul Scott Mowrer, Director of the Chicago *Daily News* Foreign Service.

i. Why We Think as We Do
ii. Difficulty of Obtaining Facts on which to Base our Opinion
iii. The Newspapers
iv. The Time-Lag in Public Opinion.

*   *   *   *   *